1. According to Ann Landers is there any-
    thing wrong with getting into the habit
    of kissing a lot of people?

Charlie Weaver: It got me out of the army!

2. Woman Magazine recommends you zip
    up the zipper of a pair of pants when
    you hang it up in the closet. Why?

Rose Marie: Modesty

3. When Stanley asked his famous question
    "Dr. Livingston, I presume?" Dr. Living-
    ston made a less famous reply. What was
    it?

Paul Lynde: "Kiss me"

Eddie LeRoy

Prior to editing HOLLYWOOD SQUARES, Gail Sicilia was Music Director at two New York City radio stations. She started her career in the broadcast departments of two advertising agencies.

She is also an avid reader, viewer and listener and is currently studying filmmaking.

Ms. Sicilia is presently producing a comedy album for the HOLLYWOOD SQUARES.

HOLLYWOOD SQUARES

Edited by Gail Sicilia

POPULAR LIBRARY • NEW YORK

1. "QUOTE-UNQUOTE"

1. According to the famous quote by Alexander Pope, a little *what* is a dangerous thing?

   PAUL LYNDE: A little pervert.

2. There's an old slang expression people use. They say: "That man is in double harness." What does that mean?

   JAN MURRAY: His hernia is worse.

3. The great writer George Bernard Shaw once wrote, "It's such a wonderful thing, what a crime to waste it on children." What is it?

   PAUL LYNDE: A whipping.

5. According to Ben Franklin, in *Poor Richard's Almanac,* "He that falls in love with himself will have no . . ." What?

PAUL LYNDE: Children.

6. It was Mark Twain who once observed that there are few of us who can stand another man's . . . something. Another man's what?

MARTY ALLEN: Advances.

7. According to the great poem by Edgar Allan Poe, "We loved with a love that was more than love, I and my . . ." I and my what?

PAUL LYNDE: Gym Teacher.

8. Charles Darwin had a theory that the mystery of man's past would be unraveled in a certain place. Where?

ROSE MARIE: A Holiday Inn.

9. Thomas Jefferson once called it the one thing that can stand by itself. What was he referring to?

CHARLEY WEAVER: 3-day-old donkey fazoo.

10. It was Aristotle who once said that even the bitterest of enemies can be united by a common . . . common what?

PAUL LYNDE: Infection.

11. The Post Office motto lists four specific things that won't stop the mailman from getting to you. Snow, rain, and heat are three of them. What's the fourth?

ROSE MARIE: A wedding band.

12. During the War of 1812, Capt. Oliver Perry made the famous statement. "We have met the enemy and . . ." And what?

PAUL LYNDE: They are cute.

13. According to an old proverb, love flies out the window when something comes in the door. When what comes in?

CHARLEY WEAVER: Her husband.

14. Albert Einstein once reflected that in his entire life he had only two really good ones. Two really good what?

CHARLEY WEAVER: McGuire Sisters.

15. Oscar Wilde once said of it, "It is the perfect type of a perfect pleasure. It is exquisite, yet it leaves you unsatisfied." What was he referring to?

MARTY ALLEN: A legitimate massage parlor.

16. According to the Dictionary of American Proverbs, what comes before pleasure?

PAUL LYNDE: The words, "Of course, I love you."

17. Billy Graham said in a recent column, "No matter how far you've let him go, your faith can end his control." What was Mr. Graham referring to?

PAUL LYNDE: A teenage boyfriend.

18. We know that Boy Scouts stick by their motto, "Be prepared." What is the Girl Scouts' Motto?

PAUL LYNDE: As long as he's prepared, they don't need a motto.

19. It was Tom Edison, the great inventor, who once commented, "The most necessary task of civilization is to teach man how to . . ." How to what?

MARTY ALLEN: How to kiss good.

20. The wise Chinese philosopher Confucius once said, "I can do absolutely nothing for the man who will not bring me his . . ." His what?

PAUL LYNDE: His number-one daughter.

2. BODY LANGUAGE

1. According to *Good Housekeeping* Magazine, what question do women ask their doctors the most?

   PAUL LYNDE: Alright, where's the nurse??

2. Within 5%, what percentage of plastic surgery patients are men?

   JAN MURRAY: Is that before or after the operation?

3. True or false: The ancient Chinese believed intense romantic encounters caused toothaches?

   PAUL LYNDE: Well then, the ancient Chinese did it wrong!

4. According to *Today's Health,* what do most dentists say you should do with your dentures when you go to bed?

CHARLEY WEAVER: Out to the home, we throw them all into the center of the room and have a swap party.

5. Rose Marie, if you had a protrusion of the maxillary incisors, where would I have to look to see it?

ROSE MARIE: How about my place, after the show?

6. According to the *Cosmo Girl's Guide to the New Etiquette,* it is "the most common cause of tooth loss among adults." What is it?

PAUL LYNDE: Adultery.

7. You're planning to go outside on a cold, wintry day and you don't want your lips to get chapped. Will lipstick protect you?

CHARLEY WEAVER: It kept me out of three wars.

8. You have a fever, chills, congestion, watery eyes, and a rash on your face and the back of your neck. Then the rash spreads all over your body. What's probably your problem?

PAUL LYNDE: Dad told me that would happen . . .

9. In order to do something that is very popular among tourists in Ireland, you must lie on your back with your head dangling below your feet, while somebody holds your knees. In order to do what?

MILTON BERLE: Kiss Maureen O'Hara.

10. Your girl friend has a bad cold. According to recent studies at Wisconsin University, are chances good that you'll catch her cold just by kissing her?

CHARLEY WEAVER: I don't know, but I'm going to try for double pneumonia.

11. In a *Vogue* Magazine article, Raquel Welch confessed that a certain part of her is artificial. It's above her shoulders. What is it?

   CHARLEY WEAVER: Above her shoulders? She must be standing on her head.

12. According to *Coronet* Magazine, as a woman grows older, what is usually the first part of her body to lose muscle tone and become flabby?

   PAUL LYNDE: The good part!

13. According to the Los Angeles *Herald Examiner,* are people more likely to have a problem with a mattress that's too soft or one that's too hard?

   ROSE MARIE: How about too empty?

14. What does Sophia Loren consider to be her greatest beauty secret?

   JAN MURRAY: Push-ups.

15. Is most of your liver above or below your waist?

   CHARLEY WEAVER: Most everything I've *got* is above my waist, Peter.

16. At sometime or another, most every woman puts something on her "cilia" to make them look nice. Where would you find a woman's cilia?

   PAUL LYNDE: I don't know, let's frisk 'er.

17. If you found a girl whose measurements were exactly the average of all the Miss Americas in history, would her bust be larger than her hips?

   CHARLEY WEAVER: Out to the home, we have the first Miss America, and her bust *meets* her hips.

18. Here's one on personality traits. Is a person who sits with one leg over the arm of a chair likely to be cooperative or uncooperative?

   PAUL LYNDE: Is this person a man or a woman?

19. We are often told not to swim after eating. According to *Today's Health*, is that a good idea or is it just an old wives' Tale?

   MARTY ALLEN: I wouldn't know about old wives' tales—I'm a leg man.

20. According to the *Los Angeles Times*, is there a very good chance that you can be struck by lightning twice and still be around to talk about it?

   PAUL LYNDE: Yes, but you talk about it in a higher voice.

21. According to Raquel Welch, a woman's bust size should have nothing to do with her sex appeal. True or false?

   JOAN RIVERS: That's easy for her to say!

22. In a recent issue of *Today's Health* Magazine, they answered an old parental question this way: "If they're no use, why not yank them out?" What were they referring to?

   PAUL LYNDE: Babies.

23. In doing traditional yoga exercises, when a person crosses his legs, entwines them under him, and tucks his heels up in his groin, what's it called?

   CHARLEY WEAVER: It's still called his groin, but it looks different.

24. According to doctors, what is the most frequently heard medical complaint?

PAUL LYNDE: Stirrups for a sore throat!!?

25. You meet a doctor at a cocktail party. Is it considered rude to ask him about his health?

ROSE MARIE: Don't ask. Just examine him.

26. Can teasing cause permanent damage to the hair?

CHARLEY WEAVER: At my age teasing damages my whole body.

27. According to a Stanford University study, who has a greater tolerance for pain, young folks or old folks?

PAUL LYNDE: I don't know yet. I'm having four more old people in tomorrow.

28. Which is lower, your kidneys or your bladder?

CHARLEY WEAVER: If you'll excuse me, I'll check my dip stick.

29. According to *Good Housekeeping,* if you want to cut down on your medical expenses, there is one thing which you should try to avoid whenever possible.

MARTY ALLEN: Bullets!

30. According to doctors, what do you have if you have "an obsessive, unrealistic fear of an external object"?

PAUL LYNDE: You've got 10 seconds to get dressed!

31. Can X-rays cause hair to grow where it didn't before?

   KAREN VALENTINE: I hope not . . . I just had a chest X-ray.

32. We all know that men have female hormones in their bodies. But does a woman have male hormones in her body?

   PAUL LYNDE: Occasionally . . .

33. According to Sexologist Dr. David Reuben, what is the most important job in the world?

   JIM BACKUS: A sexologist's assistant.

34. Dr. Norman Shumway was the first doctor in the United States to do something that has since become rather unpopular. What did he do?

   PAUL LYNDE: He sneezed during a vasectomy.

35. Among young girls, what is the most common physical problem they all share?

   MARTY ALLEN: I don't know but I wish it was me.

36. According to *Holiday Magazine,* if you're traveling across the country on a bus, why should you have sunglasses with you?

   PAUL LYNDE: Because I'm a star!

37. According to doctors, what is the best single form of insurance against heart trouble?

   PAUL LYNDE: A 78-year-old wife.

38. True or false: *Playboy Magazine* helps to support the famous Masters and Johnson Sex Institute.

   CHARLEY WEAVER: True . . . they donate the girls.

39. True or false: If you get help from a good sex therapy treatment center, it will probably cost you in the neighborhood of $2,000 per week.

    PAUL LYNDE: How much just to mingle?

40. True or false: According to doctors at the University of Toronto, a room that is kept at 60 degrees at night is better for satisfying your romantic needs.

    CHARLEY WEAVER: I, however, prefer a woman.

41. What is the first question famed sex researcher Dr. Masters asks a woman patient?

    PAUL LYNDE: Are we alone?

42. According to *Coronet Magazine*, out of every 1,000 men who have had a recent vasectomy, how many later said they wished they hadn't?

    CHARLEY WEAVER: The ones that had it done by acupuncture.

43. True or false: Sex can be fatal for a fat man.

    JAN MURRAY: No, just for his skinny wife.

44. True or false: If you are naked and inactive it takes a temperature of at least 85 degrees to keep you comfortable.

    ROSE MARIE: That's me, Peter, naked and inactive.

45. On the average, how much does your liver weigh?

    CHARLEY WEAVER: Twice as much as my onions.

46. According to *The Woman* Magazine, what is the worst enemy of a woman's skin?

    PAUL LYNDE: A fist.

47. Generally, is it more expensive for a woman to surgically have her bust made bigger or smaller?

    CHARLEY WEAVER: Well, I know at the market a cantaloupe costs more than a lemon!

48. One of Joan Crawford's beauty hints is to use mayonnaise as something. What?

    PAUL LYNDE: A negligee.

49. According to orthopedic surgeons, which situation is most likely to give you a backache: sleeping alone, or sleeping with someone else?

    CHARLEY WEAVER: I'll take my chances.

50. You're at the doctor's office, and he's examining your medula oblongata. Did you have to remove your clothes?

    ROSE MARIE: No, and I had my heart set on it!

51. Is there any medical evidence that smoking after 30 will reduce your interest in sex?

    PAUL LYNDE: After 30 what?

52. In this country today, is there a great need for new, young nurses?

    CHARLEY WEAVER: There's a great need in this very square, Peter.

53. If a person is injured, there is one thing you should never give him until he's seen a doctor. What shouldn't you give him?

PAUL LYNDE: A loan.

54. It's the middle of the night, and you're in bed. Is your blood pressure down, or is it up?

CHARLEY WEAVER: Am I alone?

55. According to an article in *Coronet* Magazine, what's the one word that explains why people undergo plastic surgery?

PAUL LYNDE: Nose.

56. If you've been working late at the office and then walk outside into the night, why should you wait a few minutes before driving off towards home?

CHARLEY WEAVER: You might get lucky.

57. If it's necessary to blow your nose in public, you should avert your head and use your handkerchief. Should you also say "excuse me"?

CHARLEY WEAVER: Only if you miss.

58. Frank Sinatra recently needed an operation. What did they operate on?

PAUL LYNDE: His stand-in.

59. According to the *Chicago Tribune*, what is nature's "last resort" in trying to keep the body warm?

JAN MURRAY: Phyllis Diller.

60. A Greek doctor named Galen invented something in 150 A.D. that millions of women still use every night. What?

PAUL LYNDE: The headache.

61. If your kid is healthy but bow-legged, should you do anything to help?

CHARLEY WEAVER: Yes, find him a knock-kneed girl.

62. Hospitals are now allowing nurses to do something because of all the leaning, reaching, and stooping the girls have to do. What are the hospitals allowing them to do?

PAUL LYNDE: Scream.

63. True or false: Right now you have more than 10 quarts of water in your body.

CHARLEY WEAVER: Yes . . . can we go to a commercial soon, Peter?

3. LEGEND AND LITERATURE

1. According to Greek legend, if a young boy was in love with a girl, he might toss something at her. And if she caught it, that meant she was receptive. What was it?

   PAUL LYNDE: His toga.

2. According to mythology, the first man was made from a tree. What was the first woman made from?

   CHARLEY WEAVER: Just a couple of drinks and a movie.

3. In mythology, what would the god Morpheus do to you while you were sleeping?

   PAUL LYNDE: I don't know about you, but I got an enchanted hickey.

4. In mythology, Hercules first showed his power when he was only eight months old by squeezing two of them in his crib. Two what?

CHARLEY WEAVER: Was his mother tucking him in?

5. In Greek mythology, Lotis, the beautiful daughter of Poseidon, was being chased by a lustful man. She prayed for help and the gods changed her into something. What?

ROSE MARIE: A bathrobe.

6. In Greek mythology, they were known as "golden apples:" What do we call them today?

JAN MURRAY: Probably silicone.

7. In mythology, Achilles' mother didn't want her son to go to war, so she dressed him up like a girl and made him sit with a bunch of women and do something. What?

CHARLEY WEAVER: The Virginia Graham Show.

8. In ancient mythology, the harpies were fierce and filthy monsters with the faces of women and the bodies of . . . what?

PAUL LYNDE: Also women!

9. In mythology, how did that legendary strong man, Hercules, finally die?

CHARLEY WEAVER: A double hernia.

10. In mythology, everything that King Midas touched turned to gold. But there was one thing he touched that made him regret ever having such power. What did he touch?

PAUL LYNDE: I know he was taking a shower . . .

11. According to the World Book, in mythology, young Ulysses did not want to go off and fight in the terrible Trojan War. So he pretended he was . . . what?

CHARLEY WEAVER: A decorator.

12. True or false: In Roman mythology, Rose Marie was the goddess of hunting.

JAN MURRAY: And still is . . .

13. According to Greek mythology, the god, Apollo, in love with the maiden, Daphne, pursued her through the forest. When he caught her, what did she change into?

MEL BROOKS: Something comfortable.

14. In mythology, Alexander the Great finally cut the legendary Gordian Knot. Then what happened?

CHARLEY WEAVER: Gordian's pants fell down.

15. What legendary beast is said to be irresistibly attracted to any beautiful, pure maiden alone in the forest?

ROSE MARIE: Burt Reynolds.

16. According to legend, only one person saw Lady Godiva ride through the streets naked. How did he make his living?

CHARLEY WEAVER: Selling photographs.

17. According to legend, he crossed America's open spaces giving seeds to strangers, planting his own, and always moving on. Who was he?

PAUL LYNDE: Hugh O'Brien.

18. There is an old superstition that if a girl goes to a wedding, then brings home something she picked up there and puts it under her pillow, she will get a man. Brings what home?

ROSE MARIE: His tuxedo.

19. There's an old superstition that if a baby is born feet first, he'll have a special talent. What talent?

PAUL LYNDE: Holding his breath for a long time.

20. According to superstition, if in your dreams you are in a strange bed, it means something. Means what?

CHARLEY WEAVER: Out to the home, that means I'm out of intensive care.

21. According to the Bible, when Lot's wife saw the wicked cities of Sodom and Gomorrah, she changed into something. What?

PAUL LYNDE: A leather jumpsuit.

22. When Noah went on the ark, did he take his wife along?

CHARLEY WEAVER: no, it was a pleasure cruise.

23. According to the Bible, Adam was supposed to "dress it and keep it." What was it?

PAUL LYNDE: A Barbie doll.

24. In the Bible, Jacob spent an entire night wrestling with someone before he learned who it was. Who was it?

MARTY ALLEN: Esther.

25. While Sampson was asleep, Delilah cut his hair off, which made him a weak man. How did Sampson regain his strength again?

PAUL LYNDE: He cut Delilah off!

26. According to Shakespeare, beauty makes a woman proud. Virtue makes her most admired. But what is it that makes a woman "seem divine"?

PAUL LYNDE: A fifth of vodka.

27. In Shakespeare, what was Juliet talking about when she said, "It is too rash, too unadvised, too sudden"?

HARVEY KORMAN: Romeo's quick little hands.

28. In what world-famous play does a queen kiss a donkey?

PAUL LYNDE: *Oh! Calcutta.*

29. What famous character described himself as "one who loved not wisely but too well"?

ROSE MARIE: Mickey Rooney.

4. JUNIOR AND SENIOR CITIZENS

1. Do unborn babies dream?

   PAUL LYNDE: Yes, about getting out!

2. According to Dr. Benjamin Spock, "It is preferable that baby not sleep in his parent's room after he is..." How old?

   ROSE MARIE: Old enough to work a camera.

3. Does standing a 5-month-old baby on his legs make him bow-legged?

   PAUL LYNDE: No. You've got to push down on him.

4. True or false: According to Dr. Benjamin Spock, a baby's body is 60% water.

   PAUL LYNDE: And the other 40% is even worse.

5. True or false: A fat mommy and a fat daddy will more than likely have a fat little baby.

   JAN MURRAY: I *know* they'd *rather* have Veal Parmigiana.

6. You have taught your baby not to hit you when he's mad. What will he probably do instead?

   PAUL LYNDE: Make an obscene gesture.

7. According to Dr. Benjamin Spock, "Most babies who use a pacifier freely for the first few months of life never become . . ." What?

   PAUL LYNDE: A leg man.

8. If you're uncomfortable about discussing sex with your child, should you do so anyway?

   MICKEY ROONEY: Sure, how else are you going to learn anything?

9. You're serving liver and onions for dinner tonight, and your young child insists over and over that he won't eat any. According to doctors in *Today's Health*, what should you do?

   PAUL LYNDE: Tell him he's adopted.

10. Your baby has a certain object which he loves to cling to. Should you try to break him of his habit?

    JOAN RIVERS: Yes, it's daddy's turn.

11. Is a Girl Scout awarded anything if she's good on roller skates?

PAUL LYNDE: I don't think it's possible on roller skates.

12. The Boy Scouts handbook advises that it's a simple task, and once it's become "a habit, it becomes part of your life and you can't help yourself" from doing it. Doing what?

CHARLEY WEAVER: Lifting the seat.

13. Can boys join the Camp Fire Girls?

MARTY ALLEN: Only after lights out.

14. When asked whether their life has been happy so far, 90% of the American youngsters polled gave the same answer. What?

PAUL LYNDE: Buzz off!

15. According to psychologists, when a child begins to get curious about sex, what is the one question he will most often ask his mommy and daddy?

PAUL LYNDE: Where can I get some?

16. According to *Ladies' Home Journal,* if your child cries out in the middle of a nightmare, is there anything you should do?

PAUL LYNDE: Soundproof his room.

17. You have a young child who has an imaginary friend he talks to, plays with, and even introduces to his friends. According to child psychologists, should you be worried about him?

CHARLEY WEAVER: Only if the imaginary friend gets pregnant.

18. If your child starts playing with his food at the table, what should you do?

   PAUL LYNDE: Push his high chair over.

19. According to Dr. Benjamin Spock, if you have twins, should you forget about nursing?

   CHARLEY WEAVER: No, but you're in trouble with triplets.

20. According to *Woman's Day*, should children always be told if they are adopted?

   PAUL LYNDE: Even if they're not. Keeps them on their toes.

21. When a couple has a baby, who is responsible for its sex?

   CHARLEY WEAVER: I'll lend him the car. The rest is up to him.

22. For many, many years, what was the person called who headed the famous "Ding Dong School"?

   PAUL LYNDE: Timothy Leary.

23. Which one of your five senses tends to diminish the quickest as you grow older?

   CHARLEY WEAVER: My sense of decency.

24. Do doctors advise elderly people to eat more slowly than younger people?

   CHARLEY WEAVER: No, hurry . . . you may never get to dessert.

25. According to *Man & Woman* Magazine, what is the main reason a 75-year-old man would marry a 70-year-old woman?

   PAUL LYNDE: He wants her body.

26. True or false: People need more and more sleep as they get older.

   CHARLEY WEAVER: It's not what they need, but it's certainly all they get.

27. According to Dr. David Reuben, can a 72-year-old woman get pregnant?

   CHARLEY WEAVER: I think she has a better shot at emphysema.

28. According to *Cosmopolitan*, what is the primary factor in determining how soon a woman turns gray?

   PAUL LYNDE: How tight you squeeze her.

29. Gloria Swanson, who is 74, says she had one in Hollywood, one in New York, one in Portugal, and one in Palm Springs. What did she have?

   ROSE MARIE: A hot flash?

30. A woman recently wrote to Dr. David Reuben asking if there was anything wrong with her 58-year-old hubby, who feels extremely amorous every single night at bedtime. What did Dr. Reuben say?

   CHARLEY WEAVER: Beg him to come back home.

31. An 80-year-old doctor in Wisconsin, A. J. Quick, has recently discovered something important and he named it after himself. What is it?

   CHARLEY WEAVER: 80 years old . . . I'd say the quickie.

32. In 1886, Grover Cleveland became the oldest of our presidents to get . . . what?

   PAUL LYNDE: Excited.

33. You're a 71-year-old man and you find that you're not interested in sex as much as you used to be. Does your doctor have something for you that might help?

   CHARLEY WEAVER: No, but his nurse does!

34. The leader of a new Senior Citizens group called the Gray Panthers says that the happiness of older people depends on two things. One of them is social reform. What's the other?

   PAUL LYNDE: A good prune crop.

35. According to a recent article in the *Miami Herald*, at age 78, is Groucho Marx still interested in sex?

   CHARLEY WEAVER: Yes, but he's forgotten the secret word.

5. PREGNANCY AND THE PILL

1. A woman you know has been trying to have a baby for the past 3 years, but she hasn't had any luck. Can hypnosis help?

   PAUL LYNDE: First I'd try dating.

2. According to recent large-scale studies on the pill in England, do women on the pill tend to be more outgoing than other women?

   CHARLEY WEAVER: If the pill works, they're out going all the time.

3. True or false: One of the side effects of the pill can be depression.

   PAUL LYNDE: Only if she forgets to take it!

4. True or false: In Italy it is against the law to send a pregnant woman to jail.

   HARVEY KORMAN: Yes, and no Italian woman has gone to jail in 28 years.

5. According to *Movie Life* Magazine, Ann-Margret would like to start having babies soon, but her husband wants her to wait awhile. Why?

   PAUL LYNDE: He's out of town.

6. You're in your mommy's tummy waiting to be born. Can you hiccup?

   REDD FOXX: Yes, but you'll give away your position.

7. Who stays pregnant for a longer period of time, your wife or your elephant?

   PAUL LYNDE: Who told you about my elephant?

8. True or false: There has been a steady decline in the birth rate in this country since 1957.

   ROSE MARIE: I've certainly done my part.

9. One woman you know takes birth control pills. Another woman doesn't take the pill. Which of them probably smokes more?

   PAUL LYNDE: Can the pill make ya' smoke?

10. According to the A.M.A., should a pregnant woman use seat belts?

    CHARLEY WEAVER: Yes. If she wants a tall, skinny child.

11. Ann Landers recently stated, "If you're pregnant, girls, do your baby a favor. Don't . . ." Don't what?

   PAUL LYNDE: Don't break up with your boyfriend.

12. A girl has been married a year and she's still not pregnant. According to *People* Magazine, should she see a doctor?

   ROSE MARIE: If he's single.

13. The famous "rabbit test" will tell you if you are pregnant. What will the "mouse test" tell you?

   PAUL LYNDE: If Annette Funicello is pregnant.

14. According to the old wives' tale, if a woman is carrying her baby high and to the right, what will she give birth to?

   MARTY ALLEN: A conservative.

15. True or false: According to *Today's Health* Magazine, orchids might be able to be used for birth control.

   PAUL LYNDE: If ya' leave the pin in.

16. Is it dangerous for a pregnant woman to use bug spray?

   CHARLEY WEAVER: It's too late, anyway.

17. Can an airline stewardess get pregnant and remain a stewardess?

   PAUL LYNDE: Yes. After a cigarette and a little nap.

18. You're taking the new "mini-pill." What will it do for you?

   PAUL LYNDE: It will ward off pygmies.

19. Who usually has a faster heartbeat, a pregnant mother or her unborn baby?

    JOHN DAVIDSON: How about the mystery father?

20. Before you are born, is it possible for you to frown?

    PAUL LYNDE: Only at strangers.

21. True or false: Scientists now believe that the moon might be used for birth control.

    PAUL LYNDE: That's hard to swallow.

6. THE BIRDS AND THE BEES, ETC.

1. What's the first thing you should do if you get stung by a bee?

   PAUL LYNDE: Swell up.

2. Why is the booby bird called the booby bird?

   KAREN VALENTINE: Because they have big . . . feet.

3. A male fly has just finished a romantic encounter. According to fly experts, what should the fly be looking forward to in the near future?

   PAUL LYNDE: I don't think he's going to do much better than another fly.

4. What is the slowest moving creature on earth?

   ROSE MARIE: The guys I go out with.

5. True or false: It is illegal in California to transport a parrot across the state line.

   PAUL LYNDE: Only if it's for immoral purposes.

6. According to the World Book, what would you call a grasshopper with short feelers?

   JAN MURRAY: Unlucky in love.

7. You are teaching your parrot to talk. Will he do better if you cover his cage, or should you leave it uncovered?

   PAUL LYNDE: Uncovered . . . so he can see my whip!

8. How often do hummingbirds mate?

   JIM BROLIN: 6,324 times a minute.

9. How does a boy firefly find a girl firefly?

   PAUL LYNDE: Trial and error.

10. What does a female moth do when she wants to attract a male?

    CHARLEY WEAVER: She eats his clothes off.

11. Studies show that eagles can do something about eight times better than humans. Do what?

    PAUL LYNDE: Make baby eagles.

12. Your pet canary is swinging in its cage, singing its heart out. Is it probably a boy canary, or a girl?

MARTY ALLEN: I can't tell . . . it's swingin' too fast.

13. Beekeepers sometimes give their bees a little nip of honey wine. Why?

PAUL LYNDE: Beekeepers are *so* lonely.

14. According to the *Los Angeles Times*, the Chinese have a very special use for hummingbird tongues. What do they use them for?

JAN MURRAY: Cheap little thrills.

15. Zoo keepers often put a sock over an ostrich's head. Why?

PAUL LYNDE: So the ostrich can't identify him in court.

16. If you had your choice, would you rather be kicked by a mule or by an ostrich?

PAUL LYNDE: They both sound pretty good to me!

7. LSD—LOVE, SEX, AND DATING

1. According to columnist Ellen Peck, if a girl goes out on a date and unexpectedly finds herself at an X-rated movie that she doesn't want to see, what should she say to her date?

PAUL LYNDE: Untie me, please.

2. You've decided that you just shouldn't continue dating this girl you've been going with for three months. According to The Playboy Advisor, where's the best place to give her the news?

CHARLEY WEAVER: Leave a note in the crib.

3. According to Dear Abby, what's the first thing a 16-year-old girl should do about a boy who won't keep his hands to himself?

JOAN RIVERS: Marry him—that's how I cured Edgar!

4. In a recent interview, Dinah Shore admitted that being in love has ruined her ability to do something as well as she once did. What can't she do as well anymore?

PAUL LYNDE: Walk.

5. According to the Encyclopedia of Etiquette, when is it not proper for a man to kiss a woman's hand?

CHARLEY WEAVER: When's she's stuffing a turkey.

6. You've given your girl friend a new angora sweater. A week later, she complains to you that it's been shedding. Is there anything you can do about it?

PAUL LYNDE: Tape her mouth shut.

7. According to Hugh O'Brien, of all the women he's dated, the one he enjoyed most was a . . . a what?

CHARLEY WEAVER: Phillipine acrobat.

8. In her advice column, Ask Karen, Karen Valentine tells a 14-year-old girl who is afraid of boys that young guys can be three things. They can be fun, they can be companions . . . and what else?

PAUL LYNDE: They can be *daddies!*

9. According to *Photoplay,* there is one thing Joe Namath doesn't like his dates to discuss. What?

BURT REYNOLDS: His passes.

10. According to columnist Ann Landers, is it okay to hold hands in the halls at school?

CHARLEY WEAVER: Not at West Point.

11. According to Dear Abby, is it wise for a woman to tell a man she loves him before he says it first?

PAUL LYNDE: If there's time.

12. You and your girl are kissing alfresco. What is alfresco?

CHARLEY WEAVER: Just an innocent bystander.

13. Newspapers in London are saying that the romance between Mark Phillips and Princess Anne is getting quite serious and that it all started because the two of them shared a common passion for something. For what?

PAUL LYNDE: Chiffon.

14. According to Joanne Woodward, there is something which, like love, "should be done and not talked about." What is it?

MEL BROOKS: Laundry.

15. True or false: John Davidson's first date when he came to Hollywood was Annette Funicello?

PAUL LYNDE. Wasn't everybody's?

16. You're a shy, bashful girl. According to *Cosmo*, will you probably be helped in overcoming your shyness by choosing an extroverted, outgoing husband?

ROSE MARIE: I did that . . . and then his wife caught us.

17. According to Dear Abby, after a young man who is dating a young woman tells her "I love you" repeatedly, there is another question she usually expects to hear next. What is it?

CHARLEY WEAVER: Shall we get back in the car?

18. In a recent interview, Tony Randall said, "Every woman I've ever been intimate with in my life was . . ." What?

   PAUL LYNDE: Bitterly disappointed.

19. According to Amy Vanderbilt, what is the maximum length of time you and your fiance should be engaged?

   ROSE MARIE: Engaged in what?

20. When you take a girl home after a date, should you offer to unlock the door for her?

   CHARLEY WEAVER: Let her find her own way out.

21. According to Amy Vanderbilt, how long should a formal engagement last?

   PAUL LYNDE: Well, check-out time's eleven.

22. You have a date with a Spanish girl, and when you pick her up, she has a duenna. What does that mean?

   CHARLEY WEAVER: Don't kiss her on the lips.

23. According to the Old Farmers' Almanac, if a man gives a woman a tulip, it means that hers are the most beautiful he has ever seen. The most beautiful what?

   PAUL LYNDE: Bulbs.

24. According to Abigail Van Buren, if a young girl would like to find out what her prospective mate is really like to live with, whom should she ask?

   JAN MURRAY: His wife.

25. According to *Coronet* Magazine, nothing confuses a man more than when a woman suddenly starts . . . starts what?

PAUL LYNDE: Before he gets there.

26. Every time you kiss your girl, you feel an irrepressible urge to laugh. Does The Playboy Advisor have any recommendations for this problem?

CHARLEY WEAVER: Try Miss September.

27. According to *Cosmopolitan*, every so often a girl will hear "the dreaded question" on a date, even if she's dating the world's greatest lover. What is the dreaded question?

PAUL LYNDE: Would you like to see my war wound?

8.   NEWSMAKERS

1. Helen Gurley Brown recently said of Henry Kissinger, "His most outstanding, endearing quality is his ability to make someone feel . . ." Feel what?

JAN MURRAY: His thighs.

2. Pat Nixon has worked at many things in her life. What was she doing when she met the President?

PAUL LYNDE: Hitchhiking.

3. Jesse L. Steinfeld is very concerned about what you eat, drink, or smoke. Why?

MARTY ALLEN: He's my mother.

4. According to Aristotle Onassis, after you've been this way for four years, nothing surprises you. What way is that?

PAUL LYNDE: Irregular.

5. Not long ago, while commenting on a very timely topic, Julie Nixon Eisenhower remarked, "Nothing could be more personal than a . . ." A what?

JAN MURRAY: Hickey.

6. Queen Elizabeth says she's had 25 years' experience with it, and she definitely thinks it's a good thing. What is it?

PAUL LYNDE: David Niven.

7. According to *Newsweek*, there's *one* thing that Ronald Reagan does not like to be called. What is it?

MARTY ALLEN: Collect.

8. Martha Mitchell recently said that she wants to work somewhere to "try to put a little love in the world." Where does she want to work to do this?

PAUL LYNDE: Sunset Boulevard.

9. Aristotle Onassis' old friend, Maria Callas, recently did something for the first time, and surprisingly didn't sing a note while doing it. What did she do?

PAUL LYNDE: Sank his yacht.

10. According to Mrs. Nixon herself, how does she want to be remembered?

CHARLEY WEAVER: As the wife of one of America's great presidents. She didn't say which one.

11. Mrs. Spiro Agnew recently published an article in *Today's Health* entitled "Don't Be Ashamed to Call Yourself . . ." What?

PAUL LYNDE: Contagious.

12. According to *Newsweek* Magazine, what one word did Julie Eisenhower say when she broke her toe recently?

JAN MURRAY: Whiplash!

13. According to the Los Angeles *Herald Examiner*, whenever Mrs. Ronald Reagan gets mad, she sits in the bathtub and talks to someone. Who?

PAUL LYNDE: George Murphy.

14. Golda Meier recently stated, "Never has a man presumed, never, to do that in my presence." Do what in her presence?

MILTON BERLE: Nipped at her brisket.

15. According to *Newsweek*, Jackie Onassis has had 19 of them in her New York apartment in the past four years. 19 what?

PAUL LYNDE: 19 of the most glorious minutes of her life.

16. Sen. Barry Goldwater recently stated, "I don't think it's a precious right, but I don't think it should be jammed down anyone's throat." What is it?

JIM BROLIN: Infidelity.

17. When Richard Nixon was Vice-President, he went someplace on a "good-will" mission but instead wound up being stoned and shouted at. Where did this take place?

PAUL LYNDE: Pat's room.

18. Princess Anne recently said, "It's the one thing the world can see I do well, and it's got nothing to do with my position or anything." What's the thing she does well?

ROSE MARIE: She ties her own shoes.

19. True or false: Virginia Knauer advises the President about consumer affairs.

JAN MURRAY: True, she's the Secretary of Hotels, Motels and Welfare.

20. Mrs. Spiro Agnew has something named "Leo" which Bob Hope gave her. What is it?

PAUL LYNDE: A son.

21. *U.S. News and World Report* said that Governor Reagan has recently been deluged with a tremendous amount of requests to do one particular thing. What is it?

SUZANNE PLESHETTE: Retire.

22. William F. Buckley, Jr. has taken lessons in something, and he claims he's pretty good at it. At what?

JIM BACKUS: Natural Childbirth.

23. According to Mrs. Harry Truman, there are two things that a woman must have to be a first lady. One is good health. What is the other?

PAUL LYNDE: A good build.

9. BOOKS, STORIES, AND COMICS

1. Chad Everett, of Medical Center, has just had a book published. What's Doc Everett's book about?

   PAUL LYNDE: The heartbreak of psoriasis.

2. One of the most popular books of recent months has been *The Sensuous Woman*, written by someone who signed her name simply, "J." What does J stand for?

   CHARLEY WEAVER: Judging by the book, she'd stand for anything!

3. Christine Jorgensen has written a book entitled *A Lump, A Pinch, and a Dash*. What is this book about?

   PAUL LYNDE: Her Sex Life.

4. According to the new book, *Those Fabulous Greeks*, as a boy, it was the first thing Aristotle Onassis saw in the morning and the last thing he saw at night. What was it?

JAN MURRAY: Maria Callas.

5. There's a popular new book out called *Please Touch*. What's it about?

CHARLEY WEAVER: Rose Marie.

6. According to the book entitled *The Art of Looking Younger,* there is one particular thing that is never, ever good for your skin, in spite of the fact that you might enjoy it. What is it?

PAUL LYNDE: A bull whip!

7. Louisa May Alcott wrote the famous book, *Little Women*. She also wrote a book about men. What was it called?

PAUL LYNDE: *What You Always Wanted to Know About Little Women But Were Afraid to Ask.*

8. Who wrote *Over the River and Into the Trees*?

VINCENT PRICE: Lassie.

9. Sex experts Masters and Johnson have been rebuked for having written a book about sex without mentioning a particular four-letter word even once. What is this word?

PAUL LYNDE: Rest.

10. There have been several books and movies about a character called Horatio Hornblower, R.N. What does R.N. stand for?

ARTE JOHNSON: Registered Nurse.

11. In a famous scene, Tom Sawyer promises his buddies he'd let them have a peek at something. What?

PAUL LYNDE: Becky Thatcher.

12. A booklet put out by Buckingham Palace warns you not to serve oysters and wine to Princess Anne. Why not?

PAUL LYNDE: She goes crazy!

13. According to the book *The Difference Between a Man and a Woman*, what is the very first trauma that a human male experiences?

JAN MURRAY: Is this male Jewish?

14. According to best-selling author Dr. David Reuben, what is the most powerful sexual instrument?

PAUL LYNDE: Unlimited cash.

15. There is a best-selling book entitled *A Man Called Lucy*. What's it about?

MARTY ALLEN: Hairdressing.

16. There's a popular new book which is subtitled *Jackie and Ari's First Year*. What's the real title of the book?

PAUL LYNDE: *It Happened one Night.*

17. According to the book *The Joy of Sex*, "Getting *something* is probably the most important lesson of sex." Getting what?

CHARLEY WEAVER: Getting *on* with it!

18. True or False: Albert Einstein and Sigmund Freud once got together and wrote a book.

    PAUL LYNDE: Yes, it was called *Sex and the Speed of Light*.

19. According to the book *Comfortable Words*, what is the most thoroughly disapproved-of word in the English language?

    ROSE MARIE: Single.

20. According to the book *How Sex Can Keep You Slim*, an average romantic session burns up how many calories? 50, 100, or 200?

    PAUL LYNDE: I don't care. I'll stick to cottage cheese.

21. Well, Dr. David Reuben has come out with a sequel to his best-selling book. The new one is called *Any Woman* ... Any woman what?

    CHARLEY WEAVER: *Will Do*.

22. According to the book *The Cowboys*, back in the Old West, where would you look to see a cowboy's jingle-bobs?

    PAUL LYNDE: Is that before or after the Indian raid?

23. Pat Nixon has written a book containing some of her memoirs called *Someone, Come Home*. Who is the someone?

    VINCENT PRICE: That's what Dick would like to know!

24. Recently, the biggest-selling book in Moscow was a bulky, 4-volume set that sold for 12 rubles. It listed 850,000 different what?

    PAUL LYNDE: Positions.

25. In *Alice in Wonderland*, what was the Queen of Hearts' favorite sport?

CHARLEY WEAVER: The Jack of Clubs.

26. With which book do you associate the expression "Big Brother is watching you"?

PAUL LYNDE: Anything by Masters and Johnson.

27. According to the book *Wake Up Your Body*, if your wife gives you a warm bath, followed by a nice, easy massage, what usually happens next?

JAN MURRAY: She'll tell you what happened to the car.

28. In the famous H. G. Wells story, "The War of the Worlds," the invading Martians are finally killed by something very small. What?

CHARLEY WEAVER: A spoonful of donkey fazoo.

29. In the popular children's Mother Goose rhyme, what did the pussy cat do under the queen's chair?

PAUL LYNDE: Numero uno.

30. In *Alice in Wonderland*, who kept crying "I'm late, I'm late"?

PAUL LYNDE: Alice . . . and her mother is sick about it!

31. In a popular children's story, who kept saying "I think I can, I think I can"?

CHARLEY WEAVER: Out to the home it's Mr. Ferguson, and Mrs. Ferguson keeps saying "I wish he would, I wish he would."

32. In a famous fairy tale, a queen is bathing when a frog jumps out of the water and says to the queen, "Thy wish shall be fulfilled." What was the queen's wish?

PAUL LYNDE: She wanted the frog to talk dirty.

33. According to a well-known Mother Goose rhyme, "Bye baby bunting, daddy's gone a-hunting to get a little..." A little what?

CHARLEY WEAVER: That's true.

34. In the story of the Christmas carol, Scrooge always said "Bah, humbug!" every time Bob Cratchit said one particular thing. What was it?

PAUL LYNDE: Kiss me.

35. What world-famous fictional character lived away from it all with an old man and a goat?

PAUL LYNDE: Jackie Onassis.

36. In the comic strips, the Green Lantern got his awesome power from a power ring and a green lamp. What was the only thing that could take his power away?

JAN MURRAY: Prune danish.

37. Superman had a large "S" on his chest. What did Captain Marvel have on his chest?

MARTY ALLEN: A training bra.

38. According to his publishers, Superman is going to undergo an image change. What will the new Superman have that he doesn't have now?

PAUL LYNDE: We won't know until they remove the bandages.

10. SEX EDUCATION AND VIOLENCE

1. According to *The Woman* Magazine, if you wake up at night and sense that there is a stranger in the room with you, what should you do?

ROSE MARIE: Rejoice!

2. According to *Coronet* Magazine, what is a man's basic sexual fear?

PAUL LYNDE: Being stuck in an elevator.

3. True or false: Most personal physical attacks are never reported to the police.

ROSE MARIE: No . . . I just put them in my diary.

4. Sigmund Freud once said that there are just two basic instincts. One, of course, is sex. What's the other?

   PAUL LYNDE: Getting some.

5. True or false: Disney Productions has made a sex-education cartoon.

   PAUL LYNDE: And guess what happens when Pinocchio tells a lie?

6. Are most sex crimes reported?

   CHARLEY WEAVER: It depends on what you call a sex crime. Out to the home, using someone else's slippers is considered a sex crime!

7. According to sex expert Dr. David Reuben, both men and women often confuse sex with one thing other than love. What do they confuse it with?

   PAUL LYNDE: Stardom.

8. What was the main source of sex education for the people who are now adults, their parents, other children, or school?

   NANETTE FABRAY: In my case, it was very thin walls.

9. According to "sexperts" Masters and Johnson, what is "The greatest form of sex education"?

   PAUL LYNDE: On-the-job training.

10. According to *Ladies' Home Journal*, if a mature man is having an affair, is he *likely* to talk about it?

    ROSE MARIE: Yes, and if he won't, I've got my own publicity man.

11. According to the Los Angeles *Herald Examiner*, does famed anthropologist Dr. Margaret Mead think that having an affair with a fellow-office worker is a good idea?

PAUL LYNDE: Yes. But unfortunately her fellow-office workers don't.

12. According to *Reader's Digest,* do "peeping devices" in the door of a girl's home help make it safer?

JIM BROLIN: It certainly makes them a lot more interesting.

13. According to *Look* Magazine, what is the best thing to do if you are confronted by a mugger?

ROSE MARIE: Find out if he's single.

14. According to Dr. David Reuben, what's the worst place in a house for a couple to discuss sexual problems?

PAUL LYNDE: The oven.

15. If you get an obscene phone call, should you attempt to reason with the caller?

ROSE MARIE: Only if he threatens to hang up!

16. You're wearing high-heeled shoes when an attacker starts coming after you. Should you run in those shoes or take them off first and then run?

ROSE MARIE: Last time it happened, I took my shoes off. It worked. All he wanted was my shoes.

17. We all know that many colleges now offer courses in sex education. Are they popular?

PAUL LYNDE: If they give ya' homework!

18. According to *Parade* Magazine, what night of the week is a woman most likely to be molested?

    ROSE MARIE: With my luck it's tonight and I'm working.

19. Researchers have found that one of the most effective methods of scaring off prowlers is something that most any woman can do. What?

    PAUL LYNDE: Have a baby.

20. According to the magazine *Sexual Behavior*, if a man attacks you, you should forget your femininity for a moment and give him a good karate chop. Where?

    ROSE MARIE: At my place.

21. If you get sex advertisements in the mail, Ann Landers advises you to write two words and the word "please" on them and drop them in a mailbox. What two words should you write?

    CHARLEY WEAVER: "Send more."

22. According to the Los Angeles Police Department, what is the best thing for a woman to do when she is walking alone, and finds that she's being followed by a man in a car?

    ROSE MARIE: Hope it's a small foreign car and head straight for the bedroom.

23. If a woman is walking alone, carrying something of value in her purse, and she sees two or more people approaching in a suspicious manner, what should she do with her purse?

    CHARLEY WEAVER: Kiss it good-bye.

24. According to police authorities, if you should ever be unfortunate enough to come face to face with a burglar, you should simply say to him, "I'll . . ." What?

PAUL LYNDE: (wink) I'll let you tie me up.

25. According to *New Woman* Magazine, if you are attacked by a mugger on the street, should you scream?

ROSE MARIE: No, he might change his mind.

26. In a recent column, Billy Graham said he would like to urge young people to reserve sex for the only place it belongs. Where is that?

PAUL LYNDE: The state prison.

27. According to police, if you are being molested, other than yelling "Help," what is the best thing to scream?

ROSE MARIE: "Encore."

11. MARRIAGE

1. In a recent survey in Sweden, young men and women were asked if they thought marriage should come before sex. What did the majority say?

   PAUL LYNDE: Help me with my blouse.

2. According to *Coronet* Magazine, there can be no meaningful marriage without it. Without what?

   ROSE MARIE: A husband!

3. The custom of putting a wedding ring on the third finger of the left hand originated because it was believed that a "vein of love" ran directly from that finger to something else. What?

   DEMOND WILSON: A Holiday Inn.

4. According to a recent Gallup Poll, do most American students favor sex before marriage?

   CHARLEY WEAVER: Most students favor it *instead* of marriage.

5. Do airline stewardesses generally make good wives?

   PAUL LYNDE: They make good wives *furious!*

6. According to a recent survey of high-school girls, what quality did they rate most important in their future hubbies?

   MARTY ALLEN: Endurance.

7. According to Abigail Van Buren, if a girl happens to be a loud snorer, should she inform her fiance of this before the wedding?

   CHARLEY WEAVER: No. With today's generation he'll already know!

8. Queen Victoria built the famous Albert Hall in London as a memorial to her husband. She built it in the shape of something you would normally find at a wedding. What is it?

   PAUL LYNDE: Lana Turner.

9. According to tradition, you can always tell a wedding ceremony is about to begin when somebody walks in and sits down. Who?

   CHARLEY WEAVER: The obstetrician.

10. The ushers at a wedding are supposed to ask a particular question of every female guest as she arrives. What's the question?

    PAUL LYNDE: "Do you mess around?"

11. According to tradition, a bride should wear something old, something new, something borrowed, and something blue. According to the poem, what should she tuck in her shoe?

STU GILLIAM: The Pill.

12. What do you call a marriage *not* performed by a clergyman?

CHARLEY WEAVER: A weekend.

13. According to *Bride's Magazine,* the groom should put it in a sealed envelope and give it to the best man who will then give it to the minister. What's in the envelope?

PAUL LYNDE: The Oscar winner for best scoring.

14. According to Dear Abby, is there a law that can force a man to marry a woman?

ROSE MARIE: Yes. It's called the *father-in-law.*

15. Can you get married in Las Vegas all night?

PAUL LYNDE: Yes . . . or by the hour.

16. According to nationwide surveys, at what age do American men think it is best to get married?

CHARLEY WEAVER: I'd say 36D. Excuse me, I over-answered.

17. We throw rice. What did the early Romans throw at weddings?

PAUL LYNDE: Orgies.

18. In East Africa, if you want to marry a girl you must first give her parents 30 to 50 of these. What are they?

ARTE JOHNSON: Grandchildren.

19. According to *Silver Screen* Magazine, Robert Young recently stated that his wife was the first girl that he ever . . . That he ever what?

PAUL LYNDE: Operated on.

20. According to *Cosmo,* if you meet a stranger at a party and you think he's real attractive, is it okay to come out directly and ask him if he's married?

ROSE MARIE: No, wait till morning.

21. Within two, how many wives did Brigham Young have?

PAUL LYNDE: All of them.

22. According to *Bride's Magazine* if a woman is saying "I do" for the second time, should she wear a veil?

CHARLEY WEAVER: What's the difference? If it's the second time, we know she does.

23. According to Dr. David Reuben, is a year of marriage long enough for the average couple to find out if their sex life will be happy?

PAUL LYNDE: Yes—then they should get back together.

24. According to surveys, do most newlyweds want to have a son or a daughter first?

JAN MURRAY: First they want to get a room.

25. Can you get married in prison?

PAUL LYNDE: If you're young and pretty.

26. According to *Cosmopolitan* Magazine, is cheating in marriage equally divided between husbands and wives?

CHARLEY WEAVER: Yes, I always took Monday, Wednesday, and Friday, and she got Tuesday, Thursday, and Saturday.

27. By law in France and Denmark, when a woman marries, she is permitted to keep something she had when she was single.

SOUPY SALES: Her little boy.

28. According to a recent study in the *American Journal of Sociology*, the more a woman has of something, the less likely she is to want to get married. What is it?

PAUL LYNDE: Male hormones.

29. True or false: In surveys of college students, one out of three say marriage is obsolete.

CHARLEY WEAVER: True. And that one should move out and leave the other two alone.

30. According to the time-honored tradition ... and Amy Vanderbilt ... at the new groom's stag party, he should lead all the other fellows in a toast to the new bride. Then what should everyone do?

PAUL LYNDE: Watch the movie!

31. According to a recent survey, there are two decisions which newlyweds consider most important. One is whether the bride should continue working. What is the other?

JAN MURRAY: Should they leave a wake-up call.

32. According to *Gentlemen's Quarterly*, is it wise to let a travel agent help with your honeymoon plans?

PAUL LYNDE: No. Three's a crowd.

33. Statistically, who watches more television, a retired couple in their sixties or a newlywed couple in their twenties?

JAN MURRAY: I'd say a newlywed couple in their sixties.

34. According to *Glamour*, who generally handles the in-laws better, the hubby or the wife?

CHARLEY WEAVER: My wife once caught me handling my sister-in-law and it took me a long time to get better.

35. True or false: Ari Onassis gave Jackie $5 million worth of jewelry in their first year of marriage alone.

PAUL LYNDE: (wink) And it didn't cure her headache.

36. Who generally has a better sense of taste, your wife or your bird?

CHARLEY WEAVER: My bird—he refuses to go near my wife.

37. You, your wife, and a lone woman guest are all at a restaurant. Whom should you seat first?

CHARLEY WEAVER: My wife, because she's all out of breath from tracking us down.

38. Princess Grace of Monaco recently admitted, "I refer to my husband as my 'leader,' and he refers to me as his . . ." What?

PAUL LYNDE: His trick.

39. According to Dear Abby, is it considered in good taste for a couple to frame their marriage certificate and hang it on the wall?

CHARLEY WEAVER: No. They might forget it when they check out.

40. According to *Women's Day* Magazine, some men are better sex partners when they reach middle age because they have lost something. What?

PAUL LYNDE: Their wives.

41. According to Emily Post, when a couple arrives at a motel, should the man go in and register alone, or should his wife accompany him?

JAN MURRAY: Seems silly to go home and get her.

42. True or false: According to the law, if a woman is elected President, her husband has to be called the First Man.

JOAN RIVERS: Only if he really was.

43. According to Cary Grant, people should get married in their early teens for one reason. Why?

PAUL LYNDE: He likes 'em young.

44. You've just married a woman who is 6 inches taller than you. According to the *Ladies' Home Journal*, does this reduce your chances for a happy marriage?

CHARLEY WEAVER: No. But it reduces *her* chances.

45. According to research, is the average runaway wife apt to be 20, 30, or 40?

MARTY ALLEN: If those are her measurements, let her go!

46. At the famous Masters and Johnson Sex Research Institute, the most-often asked question comes from wives, wanting to know one thing about their husbands. What do they ask?

PAUL LYNDE: Where is he?

47. According to marriage counselors, there are 2 words that every man and woman must learn to use if they want their marriage to work. What words are they?

JAN MURRAY: Disrobe—and that leaves me one word for later.

48. According to Dr. Joyce Brothers, women today are expected to marry men who have it over them in three ways. He should be better educated, older, and one other thing. What?

ROSE MARIE: Single.

49. If a husband has 2 wives at the same time, it's called bigamy. What is it called when a woman has 2 husbands at the same time?

PAUL LYNDE: Stereo.

50. What is the marital status of most adults in America?

CHARLEY WEAVER: Bored stiff.

51. A recent study has shown that the average woman in Japan spends more than 5 hours each day doing something, yet her husband spends only about an hour and a half doing the same thing. Doing what?

PAUL LYNDE: Makin' love.

52. Do psychiatrists consider it abnormal for a bride to cry a lot during the first few weeks of her marriage?

PAUL LYNDE: Why don't psychiatrists mind their own business?

53. According to Dear Abby, is it a wife's duty to wake her husband up in the morning?

CHARLEY WEAVER: If she knows where he's staying.

54. Julie Nixon Eisenhower recently said that the only time she cried since she's been married is when David beat her. At what?

PAUL LYNDE: At home.

55. True or false: According to statistics, married people make better drivers than single people.

MARTY ALLEN: True. Because married people are in the front seat.

56. According to Dear Abby, what should you do if you suspect, but cannot prove, that your husband is trying to kill you?

CHARLEY WEAVER: Buy a bulletproof nightie.

57. Is there anything a wife can legally do if her husband refuses to repay money that she lent him?

PAUL LYNDE: Cut off his . . . privileges.

58. Can children wreck a happy marriage?

CHARLEY WEAVER: No. But they can foul up a casual acquaintance.

59. According to Dr. Joyce Brothers, "It has replaced sex as the greatest emotional and marital disturbance." What is it?

PAUL LYNDE: A good punch in the mouth.

60. Is Mickey Rooney married right now?

JAN MURRAY: What time is it?

61. According to the *Los Angeles Citizens News*, sex is one of the two major causes of divorce. What is the other?

JIM BROLIN: No sex.

62. According to Alfred Hitchcock, after a few years of marriage, what everyday thing often takes the place of sex?

PAUL LYNDE: Your wife.

63. According to Tennesee law, a man cannot divorce his wife unless he leaves her 10 pounds of dried beans, 5 pounds of dried apples, and a year's supply of . . . what?

PAUL LYNDE: Field hands.

64. According to the popular new book on divorce called *Starting Over*, there's a big surprise waiting for the person who suddenly finds himself single again. What is it?

CHARLEY WEAVER: Rose Marie.

65. According to *Coronet* Magazine, it "really bugged" Frank Sinatra when Mia Farrow refused to take something from him. What did she refuse to take?

PAUL LYNDE: Frank Junior.

66. True or false: Under old Roman law, a man could divorce his wife merely by telling her he was doing so in the presence of 7 witnesses.

CHARLEY WEAVER: Or if *she* was doing it in the presence of 7 witnesses.

67. According to Rona Barrett's *Hollywood*, Jane Brolin says that her husband Jim always wanted to do it, but she doesn't know if he'll ever try it in front of an audience. Try what?

PAUL LYNDE: Cheating.

68. According to court records, when a couple that only has one car gets a divorce, who usually gets the car?

JOAN RIVERS: The wife gets *part* of the car. The husband gets the shaft.

69. According to Dear Abby, if a wife catches her husband fooling around, should she give him another chance?

PAUL LYNDE: Sure. Practice makes perfect.

70. Who has the most trouble getting to sleep, bachelors, married men, or divorced men?

ROSE MARIE: . . . I'm trying to remember.

71. According to the mail Dear Abby receives, what is the number-one cause of friction between married couples?

PAUL LYNDE: Burlap sheets?

72. Traditionally, an Arab husband can divorce his wife by saying something three times. What?

JAN MURRAY: I love my camel.

73. If your marriage counselor looks uncomfortable when you're discussing your problems with him, what should you do?

PAUL LYNDE: Get dressed and leave.

74. True or false: Medical studies show that the longer a man and a woman are married to each other, the more their bodies tend to act like each other's.

CHARLEY WEAVER: I know *Mr.* Ferguson nursed their last child.

75. True or false: An appropriate gift for your first wedding anniversary is something made out of plastic.

PAUL LYNDE: Either that or the pill.

76. According to Amy Vanderbilt, there are *two* gifts that are most appropriate for a sixtieth wedding anniversary. One is diamonds. What's the other?

ROSE MARIE: Batteries.

77. Ari Onassis once promised Jackie, "I will tell you everything I know, except for one thing. I will never tell you . . ." What?

PAUL LYNDE: My height.

12. FACTS AND FIGURES

1. Has sex been around for more than a billion years?

   CHARLEY WEAVER: As far as I know it went into hiding about 30 years ago.

2. True or false: Roses will last longer if you put a little sugar in their water.

   ROSE MARIE: I don't know, but if you freshen my drink I can last all night.

3. True or false: By law, women in the military cannot bear arms, are not trained to handle weapons, and may not serve in combat situations.

   PAUL LYNDE: There's only one thing left!

4. Is there a weight limit for bags on airline flights in this country?

   CHARLEY WEAVER: If she can fit under the seat, she can fly.

5. There is a force that pulls a body outward when it is moving in a circle. What do we call it?

   PAUL LYNDE: A living bra.

6. According to the World Book, what will a new Marine in boot camp hear every night at 10 P.M.?

   GEORGE GOBEL: "Do you find me attractive?"

7. Einstein's theories hold that nothing in the universe can ever move faster than one particular thing. What?

   PAUL LYNDE: A Mexican food taster!

8. True or false: According to a study in the magazine, *Psychology Today*, put a group of strangers in a dark room for 90 minutes and eventually they will start feeling affectionate towards each other.

   MARTY ALLEN: What took so long?

9. In 1944, President Roosevelt signed the Servicemen's Readjustment Act, which became better known by what other name?

   JOAN RIVERS: The June Taylor Dancers.

10. True or false: About 25 percent of all fatal fires in the home start in the bedroom.

    CHARLEY WEAVER: Out to the home, that's the *only* thing that starts in the bedroom.

11. You're lying on the bed in a supine position. Can you see the ceiling?

PAUL LYNDE: Am I alone?

12. According to the laws of science, if something isn't a gas or a solid what is it?

CHARLEY WEAVER: Out to the home, it's a false alarm!

13. Before you go to bed at night, you clamp a new invention on the back of your head that gouges you with 60 tiny plastic spikes if you roll over on your back. What is the new invention supposed to prevent?

ROSE MARIE: Babies.

14. How long, at the outside, should it take you to make a bed?

ARTE JOHNSON: I don't know. . . . My bed's inside.

15. During a tornado, are you safer in the bedroom or in the closet?

ROSE MARIE: Peter, unfortunately I'm always safe in the bedroom.

16. True or false: Spanking is legal in Los Angeles schools.

PAUL LYNDE: Yes, but only between consenting adults.

17. Do scientists have a *special* word for something that lasts only one-billionth of a second?

CHARLEY WEAVER: Out to the home, it's called hanky-panky.

18. True or false: There is an unmistakable shortage of fertilizer in America this year.

    VINCENT PRICE: Not according to *T.V. Guide*.

19. According to the Internal Revenue Service, is it ever possible for you to claim your great-grandmother as a tax exemption?

    PAUL LYNDE: Yes, but hurry!

20. True or false: The majority of Americans have never spent even one night in a hotel.

    CHARLEY WEAVER: Most of us have spent a few hours, though.

21. Within two inches . . . how tall is Aristotle Onassis?

    ROSE MARIE: Standing on his wallet?

22. In an average year, California has 200 of them. 200 what?

    PAUL LYNDE: Successful marriages.

23. Two people named Gregg and Pitman have helped secretaries the world over keep their bosses happy. What did Gregg and Pitman do?

    SALLY STRUTHERS: They invented the Hide-a-Bed.

24. Is it illegal to use a false name when you check into a hotel?

    CHARLEY WEAVER: If it is, I'm wanted in 27 states.

25. You are sinking in quicksand. According to the World Book, what is the first thing you should do?

PAUL LYNDE: Disrobe and hope you'll attract a crowd.

26. True or false: You've spent about a third of your life in bed.

ROSE MARIE: Then it better work out to be the last third.

27. True or false: It's against the law in New York to sell alligator shoes.

ROSE MARIE: You can't sell them drinks, either.

28. True or false: No girl with more than a 37-inch bust has ever won the Miss America Pageant.

CHARLEY WEAVER: True, but one came in second . . . and third.

29. Scientists describe it this way: "The excitation of surface nerves due to light stimulation, causing reactions of uneasiness or spasmodic movement." What do we call it?

PAUL LYNDE: Levis.

30. How often do you celebrate a sexennial?

CHARLEY WEAVER: Not too often, anymore.

13. MAN'S BEST FRIENDS

1. Can a Chihuahua have a nervous breakdown?

   PAUL LYNDE: If he's in love with a Great Dane.

2. Your dog has been having some trouble finding the newspaper you spread out for him. Is it possible he needs glasses?

   CHARLEY WEAVER: If he misses the newspaper, he'd never hit a glass.

3. According to authority Dr. Peter Steincrohn, is it a bad idea to kiss your dog on the mouth?

   PAUL LYNDE: It seems only natural after petting.

4. Does a dog have a need for privacy?

   MEL BROOKS: Yes, but they'll settle for a tree.

5. What do we call a cat with blue eyes; a small head; cream-colored body; and chocolate face, legs, and tail?

   PAUL LYNDE: A tap dancer.

6. If you see your pet dog chewing on the grass in your back yard, is that a sign that he's not feeling well?

   CHARLEY WEAVER: No, but if you catch him *smoking* the grass . . .

7. True or false: There is a dating service in Los Angeles designed exclusively for dogs.

   ROSE MARIE: That explains my last date!

8. When your pet male fish starts blowing bubbles in his aquarium, what does it mean?

   CHARLEY WEAVER: No more Mexican fish food.

9. When a dog is happy that you've just arrived home, he'll wag his tail. What will a goose do?

   PAUL LYNDE: Make him bark.

10. Dalmatians have been known as fire dogs for a long time. Did Dalmatians ever really help put out a fire?

    CHARLEY WEAVER: Maybe a small brush fire.

14. NAME DROPPING

1. Eddie Fisher recently told an interviewer, "What I want to do now is . . ." What does he want to do now?

   PAUL LYNDE: Give Liz one more chance.

2. What famous star recently said, "I'm the only star in T.V. with a complete male and female wardrobe"?

   JIM BROLIN: Do you want them in alphabetical order?

3. Something belonging to Frank Sinatra recently caught fire. Fortunately, none of the 6 people inside it was injured. What was it that caught fire?

   PAUL LYNDE: His sleeping bag.

4. True or false: According to Holywood columnist Doris Lilly, Sophia Loren will only allow one side of her face to be photographed. Which side?

MEL BROOKS: The inside, but you need a very small camera.

5. There is one word that has been closely associated with Lawrence Welk for a long time, and in a recent, brief, "Candid Viewer" interview, he said it 9 times. What word is it?

PAUL LYNDE: Laxative.

6. Actress Jill St. John recently said that Henry Kissinger has the most fabulous one she's ever encountered. What was she referring to?

MARTY ALLEN: She didn't say.

7. According to Jimmy Stewart, he used to date Olivia de Havilland, but he had to stop going out with her because he couldn't introduce her to people. Why not?

PAUL LYNDE: His wife had no sense of humor.

8. According to Burt Reynolds, women reach their best after what?

ROSE MARIE: Three martinis.

9. Liz Taylor refers to it as "the fat one." What is it?

PAUL LYNDE: They both look the same to me!

10. True or false: Mae West will soon appear in the centerfold of *Playboy* Magazine.

JAN MURRAY: False. *Playboy* Magazine will soon appear in the centerfold of Mae West.

11. According to Jackie Onassis's former masseuse, does Aristotle spoil her?

   PAUL LYNDE: Only when Jackie's away.

12. What does Britain's Princess Anne say is the great love of her life?

   VINCENT PRICE: Sal Mineo.

13. Pat Nixon recently stated, "He's so much fun." Who was she referring to?

   PAUL LYNDE: That's what Dick would like to know.

14. According to columnist Dorothy Manners, "Zsa Zsa and Eva Gabor have probably not made one in their entire lives." Made what?

   ROSE MARIE: About the only thing I can think of would be a Viking.

15. Cary Grant admitted recently that rather than be hounded by women seeking autographs, he sometimes gives them a ... A what?

   PAUL LYNDE: A peek.

16. According to Robert Mitchum, one thing has ruined more actors than drink. What is it?

   JIM BROLIN: Otto Preminger.

17. Advice columnist Ann Landers says that when she hears those "four-letter words" in mixed company, they make her feel a certain way. What way is that?

   PAUL LYNDE: All tingly.

18. True or false: A rumored romance is being reported between Mama Cass Elliot and Don Knotts.

LILY TOMLIN: True. She left him flat and he can't get get over her.

19. John Wayne recently stated, "I try to do my best for my country, but I consider myself really an expert only when it comes to . . ." What?

PAUL LYNDE: Maureen O'Hara.

20. Candice Bergen recently stated, "It's tough for me *not* to like a man who is . . ." Who is what?

ROSE MARIE: Available.

21. When David Janssen was introduced to President Nixon recently, the President said to him, "I loved you in the . . ." In the what?

PAUL LYNDE: . . . the silly dream I had.

22. According to the *Detroit Sunday News*, Redd Foxx keeps something in his living room that reminds him of Christmas. What is it?

JOAN RIVERS: A girl named Mary.

23. According to Hugh Hefner, at what time does he usually go to bed?

PAUL LYNDE: At 6 P.M., and 8 P.M., and 11 P.M.

24. Lana Turner recently announced that she's going to franchise a chain of them. Of what?

VINCENT PRICE: Wedding chapels.

25. According to Suzanne Pleshette, first she considers herself a wife. What does she consider herself second?

PAUL LYNDE: Unfaithful.

26. The Rev. Billy Graham was once offered something by Cecil B. DeMille, but he turned it down. Most people would have jumped at it. What was it?

PAUL LYNDE: Paulette Goddard.

27. Is Douglas Fairbanks, Jr. a knight?

JIM BROLIN: He's hardly an evening anymore.

28. Aristotle Onassis recently told a gossip columnist that "anyone circulating this story will be sued by Mrs. Onassis and myself for publishing false and malicious rumors." What story was it?

PAUL LYNDE: I can't tell you. They'll sue me.

29. Pearl Bailey recently spoke to the President for 40 minutes, then he reminded her that the last time she visited him, she took home something odd as a souvenir. What was it?

STU GILLIAM: The Ambassador from Liberia.

30. According to Robert Redford, man's greatest weakness can be summed up in one word. What word?

PAUL LYNDE: Hernia.

31. Lawrence Welk says that as a young boy he once went trapping for wild animals, and when he sold the skins and got fifteen dollars, he went out and bought his first one. His first what?

JAN MURRAY: Lennon Sister.

32. Jack Lord, of "Hawaii Five-O," recently stated, "You can't live in Hawaii very long without picking up a lot of . . ." What?

PAUL LYNDE: Sailors.

33. According to Anthony Quinn, "If I don't *blank* during a day, I can't eat or make love." What does Quinn have to do during a day in order to eat or make love?

PAUL LYNDE: Beg.

15. DRESSED OR UNDRESSED

1. In a recent survey, people were asked if they would take off all their clothes in public for $1 million, what did the majority say?

   CHARLEY WEAVER: You're standing on my shorts.

2. In mythology, somebody famous slew the Queen of the Amazons and took her girdle. Who was it?

   PAUL LYNDE: The Earl of Fetish.

3. A woman you know tells you that her bra size seems to change a little about every 6 months. Is that pretty unusual?

   CHARLEY WEAVER: Out to the home, it's not unusual. It's not even pretty!

4. According to Dr. David Reuben, can a woman with a 29AAA Bra size somehow manage to nurse a baby?

   PAUL LYNDE: Yes, but stand by with a sandwich.

5. According to the Los Angeles *Herald*, if a woman's girdle is too tight, what may she develop?

   JOAN RIVERS: A very large bosom.

6. Is there any such thing as an F cup, in bra sizes?

   PAUL LYNDE: Yes, it sleeps four.

7. Why do medical experts say that women should not wear a girdle when going outdoors in very cold weather?

   CHARLEY WEAVER: Because it's not as warm as a coat.

8. True or false: Many people sleep better in their street clothes than they do in their pajamas.

   PAUL LYNDE: Yes. We call them winos.

9. According to *Good Housekeeping,* how many years is the life expectancy of your negligee?

   ROSE MARIE: If you're talking about wear and tear, mine will last forever.

10. According to *Gentlemen's Quarterly,* what is the number-one threat to masculine vanity?

    PAUL LYNDE: See-through slacks.

11. A nationwide survey of personnel directors was recently taken, and they were asked if they would hire a girl who showed up for an interview in a see-through blouse. What did most of them say?

PAUL LYNDE: Bring her in!

12. A recent study has shown that you will always get much faster service in a department store if you do one thing to attract the clerk's attention. What should you do?

MARTY ALLEN: Disrobe.

13. Are there any nudist camps in Italy?

PAUL LYNDE: No. The flies would eat ya' alive.

14. Are most people who go to nudist camps married?

CHARLEY WEAVER: No. But I've seen several of them engaged.

15. It is considered in bad taste at nudist camps to discuss two subjects. One is politics. What is the other?

PAUL LYNDE: Tape measures.

16. True or false: Whistler's famous mother once blew her top when she caught her son painting the family maid in the nude.

CHARLEY WEAVER: Well, he was using a hand roller.

17. Nudist camps often advertise that they offer the "3 R's." Two of them are rest and relaxation. What is the third "R" of nudist camps?

PAUL LYNDE: Reddi-Whip.

18. Are there any pockets in a Scotsman's kilts?

PAUL LYNDE: Eventually.

19. About two-thirds of the leather made in the United States today is used to make . . . what?

PAUL LYNDE: Party favors.

20. True or false: According to Earl Wilson, Liberace has a floor-length ermine coat in his closet that was originally designed for Queen Elizabeth.

RICH LITTLE: Who got the pumps?

21. According to Sally Struthers, she wears loud clothing because of one of her physical characteristics. Which one?

PAUL LYNDE: Her left one.

22. What do these four names bring to mind? Captain Molyneaux, Dorian, Adrian and Chanel?

ROSE MARIE: One of the most wonderful weekends I've ever spent.

23. In lots of his movies, Michael Caine wears something that very few heroes like to be seen in. What?

PAUL LYNDE: A peignoir.

24. According to a recent letter in her column, does Dear Abby approve of tight pants?

MARTY ALLEN: No, they make her cough.

25. What would you expect to find under a cowboy's chaps?

PAUL LYNDE: I bet I'm disappointed.

26. Is the Gibson Girl skirt above or below the ankles?

CHARLEY WEAVER: That depends on what the Gibson Girl is doing.

27. What's the first thing you should do when you remove your bathing suit?

PAUL LYNDE: Tell her you love her.

28. True or false: According to the *National Tattler,* fur experts say that it's a good idea, every so often, to run your hands over your favorite fur coat.

CHARLEY WEAVER: And also the gentleman who bought it for you.

29. According to Amy Vanderbilt, is a 19-year-old too young to wear mink?

PAUL LYNDE: If he's old enough to be drafted, he's old enough to wear mink.

16. FOOD

1. True or false: Food makes you sexy and sex makes you hungry.

   PAUL LYNDE: Yes. It's a vicious circle!

2. To the ancient Romans, it was the most prized and precious fruit of all. Which fruit is it?

   VINCENT PRICE: Augustus Caesar.

3. According to a recent survey, three out of four Frenchmen who eat in restaurants will always ask the owner his opinion of something. Of what?

   PAUL LYNDE: Their wife.

4. **Are** watermelons popular in Italy?

   CHARLEY WEAVER: Well, Sophia's a big star there.

5. According to the Bible, if Adam and Eve had eaten fruit from the tree of life, they would have been able to do something forever. What?

   PAUL LYNDE: Avoid irregularity.

6. According to *Redbook*, what is the best month for putting up your strawberry preserves?

   JIM BACKUS: Putting them up where, Peter?

7. When Stanley was looking for Livingston in Africa, he said, "You only eat it if you're out of all other food." Eat what?

   PAUL LYNDE: A Watusi.

8. You are in a place that produces more prunes and plums than all the rest of the country combined. What state are you in?

   CHARLEY WEAVER: Ecstasy.

9. According to the World Book, is it okay to freeze your persimmons?

   PAUL LYNDE: No. You should dress warmly.

10. According to the California Raisin Advisory Board, are the little wrinkled things abundant or is there a shortage?

    CHARLEY WEAVER: Out to the home, there's an abundance of little wrinkled things. We also have some raisins!

11. Did the ancient kings of Egypt know what a pear was?

    PAUL LYNDE: Yeah! Cleopatra showed 'em.

12. True or false: Rubbing grapefruits on your body makes you sexy.

MARTY ALLEN: Whose grapefruits?

13. If you eat a lot of prunes, will you get a fair supply of vitamins?

CHARLEY WEAVER: Yes, but you'll have to order them by phone.

14. According to the Bible, when three angels came to Abraham's tent, he offered them something that was considered a delicacy in those days. What was it?

PAUL LYNDE: Naomi.

15. It's the size of a grapefruit, it weighs about three pounds, and you have one. What is it?

JAN MURRAY: How many does Raquel Welch have?

16. Why is it smart to drop oranges into hot water for a few minutes before squeezing them?

PAUL LYNDE: Show 'em who's boss!

17. According to food experts, there are things you should do to an item when shopping. First look at it. Then feel it. What do you do to it next?

JAN MURRAY: Buy it a drink.

18. According to *Vogue*, the smartest new dinner parties are being called "moveable feasts." What is a moveable feast?

CHARLEY WEAVER: Prune Cacciatore.

19. According to French Chef Julia Child, how much is a pinch?

PAUL LYNDE: Just enough to turn 'er on.

20. True or false: When opening a bottle of champagne, you should try to uncork it with the minimum pop possible.

CHARLEY WEAVER: Only if her husband's asleep.

21. Can you get cheese from a water buffalo?

PAUL LYNDE: Only at gunpoint.

22. Every night your wife covers her face with yogurt. Is that beneficial?

CHARLEY WEAVER: It helps, but I can still tell it's her.

23. What's the correct word for a place where only butter and cheese are made?

PAUL LYNDE: A convent.

24. In order to make Chicken Tetrazzini properly, you have to remove something from the chicken first. What?

PAUL LYNDE: The rooster.

25. After baking a chicken, is it okay to leave it in a cool oven overnight?

MEL BROOKS: This is an excellent way to housebreak a chicken.

26. In preparing Chicken à la King or Chicken Kiev, what is the first thing you should do to the chicken?

PAUL LYNDE: Tip-toe up behind it with a hammer.

27. In terms of calories, does it make much of a difference if you remove the chicken's skin before cooking it?

   JIM BROLIN: It does to the chicken!

28. Is it okay to stuff a goose with prunes?

   PAUL LYNDE: Yes, but don't let it fly.

29. According to an article in *Cosmopolitan* Magazine, is hot chicken soup an aphrodisiac?

   MARTY ALLEN: Not if you spill it on your pajamas.

30. You're at the supermarket, checking out the clams. You tap the shell of one clam and it closes tightly. What does this mean?

   PAUL LYNDE: She's not in the mood.

31. What did it mean in the 16th century when a woman slept with a milk-soaked veal cutlet on each cheek?

   MARTY ALLEN: Same as it does today, Pete. . . . She's bananas.

32. During the Middle Ages and for hundreds of years after, what was the main food of the German peasant?

   CHARLEY WEAVER: The Hungarian peasant.

33. There's only one authentic way to make beef jerky. How?

   PAUL LYNDE: Hide his lady friend.

34. True or false: In the early 1900s, the United States Senate passed a resolution which required the Senate dining room to serve bean soup every day.

   CHARLEY WEAVER: And we've never heard the end of it!

35. According to *Family Circle*, to be safe, the best place to keep it is in a plastic bag in the bottom of an empty cereal box and then cover it over with cereal. What is it?

PAUL LYNDE: Your first-born.

36. Take strong black coffee with a dash of sugar. Lace it with whiskey and top with whipped cream. What's that?

CHARLEY WEAVER: Breakfast. Next question.

37. According to *Women's Wear Daily*, cooking expert Julia Child does something to every reporter who interviews her. What does she do?

PAUL LYNDE: You mean during the 20 minutes while the pot roast is cooling?

38. According to Sophia Loren, is she very good in the kitchen?

JIM BROLIN: Yes—and also in the hall.

39. In Mexico, it's very easy to get something called "sangrita." What do you do with it once you get it?

CHARLEY WEAVER: Nothing—it goes away in five days.

40. According to *The New York Times*, the increase in pollution is causing more and more Americans to drink something. What?

PAUL LYNDE: Anything.

17. WHO, WHAT, WHERE

1. In England, they're often referred to as "solicitors." What are they called here?

   PAUL LYNDE: Models.

2. According to *Coronet* Magazine, what one room in your house is the center of environmental pollution and waste?

   CHARLEY WEAVER: My bedroom.

3. You're looking for a souvenir in Holland, and a man offers you his "klompen." What does that mean?

   JOAN RIVERS: I don't know about Holland, but in this country it's 1-10! (years)

4. According to the column "Hints from Heloise," what is the most common cause of holes in your bed sheets?

PAUL LYNDE: French heels.

5. If your "stem hubs" are too thin, you have "broken jewels," and your "crown head" is stripped, where would you go to get them fixed?

CHARLEY WEAVER: A private hospital in Denmark.

6. One of the most famous paintings by the French artist Renoir is called two girls at . . . at what?

VINCENT PRICE: At once.

7. They are happy, co-operative, and industrious and their slogan is "give service." Who are they?

PAUL LYNDE: The Rockettes.

8. Now England calls her "The Queen Mother." What was she called back in 1938?

CHARLEY WEAVER: The Queen Pregnant.

9. Early man used to make his bed out of leaves. What did he usually cover his bed with?

PAUL LYNDE: Early woman?

10. Your job requires you to work from eleven at night until seven in the morning. What's that commonly called?

JAN MURRAY: Cheating.

11. There is an organization of people from all over the world called the Baker Street Irregulars who are all interested in the same thing. What?

PAUL LYNDE: Milk of Magnesia.

12. Three different types are the "lean-to," the "wedge," and the "crawl-in." What are they?

    CHARLEY WEAVER: Suggestions from Masters and Johnson.

13. If you are visiting one of the famous Seven Sisters on the East Coast, what would you be visiting?

    MILTON BERLE: A cheap motel.

14. What is the title for the person who advises students at a college?

    PAUL LYNDE: Obstetrician.

15. The newest addition to Madame Tussaud's Famous Wax Museum is a statue of Jackie and Ari Onassis. Ari is sitting on an airplane. What is Jackie sitting on?

    CHARLEY WEAVER: Ari.

16. When a member of the President's Cabinet resigns, he traditionally gets to take something back home that had been close to him during his time of duty. What is it?

    NANETTE FABRAY: His secretary.

17. Two space ships meet out there in space. Now they slowly come together and finally touch each other. What is this called?

    PAUL LYNDE: Foreplay.

18. They come linked together, and three common types are "twisted," "straight," and "stud." What are they?

    JAN MURRAY: The King Family.

19. If a sailor has a "forty-eight," what does he have?

    PAUL LYNDE: A spectacular date.

20. On an ocean liner what do you call the person who takes care of your valuables?

    CHARLEY WEAVER: In my case, the ship's doctor.

21. If you used the word "condominium" around Julius Caesar, would he have understood what you were talking about?

    PAUL LYNDE: He would have washed my mouth out with soapium.

22. The diamond is the hardest precious stone in the world. What comes after the diamond?

    JAN MURRAY: A weekend in Acapulco.

23. According to *The Wall Street Journal,* the rate of exchange of the Mexican peso hasn't changed since 1954. In terms of U.S. money, it's still worth about what?

    HARVEY KORMAN: Five minutes.

24. *Time* Magazine describes it as "a vinyl bag filled with water and fitted out with a temperature-control device." It feels like a "huge warm hand." What is it?

    PAUL LYNDE: Sounds like mom!

25. What is the organization "Cooperative for American Relief Everywhere" better known as?

    CHARLEY WEAVER: The Prune Advisory Board.

26. If you put your thumbs in your ears, pinch your nose closed with your little fingers, and sip a glass of water, what are you doing?

MARTY ALLEN: Practicing birth control.

27. Engineers in Detroit predict that several small knobs on the dashboard of your car will eventually replace something. What?

PAUL LYNDE: Your date.

28. We've all heard of leap year. Is there any such thing as a leap minute?

CHARLEY WEAVER: Out to the home, that's love.

29. The name for this well-known room comes from the Greek word meaning "to exercise naked." What do we call it?

PAUL LYNDE: Delivery room.

30. What caused the loudest noise heard in recorded history?

PAUL LYNDE: Lunch at the Acapulco Hilton.

31. A survey of travel agents has determined the seven man-made wonders of the U.S.A. Name any one of them.

McLEAN STEVENSON: Raquel Welch.

32. The largest one in the world is located in Moscow and can accommodate 6 thousand people at a time. What is it?

PAUL LYNDE: Catherine the Great!

33. According to *Ladies' Home Journal,* this event has been defined as "the blur between brushing one's teeth and starting the car." What is this event called?

ROSE MARIE: Marriage.

34. What would you be looking for if you were out shopping for flatware?

JAN MURRAY: A blouse for Phyllis Diller.

35. According to *Cosmopolitan,* you should never borrow anything from a friend if it is . . . what?

PAUL LYNDE: Under 18.

36. According to government statistics, where will you find the wettest spot in the world?

CHARLEY WEAVER: Wherever you scare an elephant.

37. If your job requires you to spend your day working with joints, trusses, and studs, then you are probably . . . what?

PAUL LYNDE: A towel boy.

38. When Miss Venus Ramey won the Miss America title in 1944, she set the record for bust measurement, which still stands (37½). She also had something else that no other Miss America has ever had. What?

CHARLEY WEAVER: Very poor posture.

39. After its last six months, it recorded 175,000 lost people, 55 weddings, 141 arrests for being drunk, and one little boy was born. Where?

JAN MURRAY: The Dean Martin Show.

40. Many sociologists suggest that one way to make people drive more carefully is to put something on their license plates. What?

PAUL LYNDE: Their kids.

41. They call themselves "Jockettes." Who are they?

PAUL LYNDE: Boy Rockettes.

42. A mermaid is a girl who is half woman and half fish. What is the proper word for a man who is a fish from the waist down?

MARTY ALLEN: Single.

43. According to the *Los Angeles Times*, movie stars are known for having them, and one out of four people in Washington, D.C. has one. What are they?

PAUL LYNDE: Affairs.

44. According to *Redbook* Magazine, they should always be stored with the broad end up. What were they referring to?

PAUL LYNDE: Ozzie and Harriet.

45. According to the *Omaha World Herald*, there are just 88 known active and semi-active ones in the world. What are they?

CHARLEY WEAVER: Out to the home, that would be kidneys.

46. In Canada, what do they call a five-cent piece?

   CHARLEY WEAVER: Yukon Lil.

47. You are riding along in the "tubes." Just where are you?

   PAUL LYNDE: I think I'm about to be born!

18. MALE OR FEMALE

1. According to psychologists, who tend to discuss the opposite sex more: men or women?

   PAUL LYNDE: Did you say discuss or disgust?

2. Can you tell the difference between a man's snore and a woman's snore?

   CHARLEY WEAVER: No. And it's gotten me into a lot of trouble, Pete. •

3. According to *Pageant* Magazine, generally, do men tend to get into bed the same way women do?

   MARTY ALLEN: If we did, *we'd* be wearin' minks.

4. True or false: Today, one out of every three plastic surgery patients is a man.

   PAUL LYNDE: Before . . . or after?

5. According to the most recent studies available, who's more apt to insist that sex be accompanied by a serious, meaningful relationship: the boy or the girl?

   JIM BROLIN: I would say the girl's father.

6. If a man gives a great performance, it's customary to yell "Bravo!" What should you yell out if a woman gives a great performance?

   PAUL LYNDE: "Mind if I smoke?"

7. According to experts, probably the easiest way for a man to appear more handsome and youthful to the opposite sex is to do something. Do what?

   JAN MURRAY: Flash a roll of hundreds.

8. Ann Landers says she knows what a real man is. How does she know?

   PAUL LYNDE: She peeked!

9. According to sexologist Dr. David Reuben, what is the one quality a woman needs most to give her sex appeal?

   CHARLEY WEAVER: Her own apartment.

10. According to the *Herald Examiner*, for every $5 earned by a man on a certain type of job, how much can a woman expect to earn in a similar job?

    PAUL LYNDE: If she's really built, about $50.

11. What do you call a man who's the head of a monastery?

    MARTY ALLEN: Unlucky in love.

12. True or false: as far as the U.S. goes, there are more women smugglers than men.

    CHARLEY WEAVER: Well, they have more places to hide things.

13. According to Richard Burton, the best way to handle a woman is to give her something. What?

    PAUL LYNDE: A bath.

14. Back in the 1880s, young boys, usually teenagers, were the primary source of telephone operators. But by 1890, they were being replaced by girls. Why?

    MILTON BERLE: Do you know a third choice, Peter?

15. Do most men think it's sexy when a woman adjusts their neckties?

    PAUL LYNDE: How tight?

16. According to the *Ladies' Home Journal*, what is the main reason that more men aren't secretaries?

    MARTY ALLEN: Bad legs.

17. During a weekend of skiing, who's more likely to have an accident: a man or a woman?

    PAUL LYNDE: On the slopes . . . or in the lodge?

18. Are there any women on the F.B.I.'s latest "Ten Most Wanted" list?

CHARLEY WEAVER: Just one, and her phone never stops ringing.

19. According to Dr. Joyce Brothers, who is usually the closest confidant of an unmarried young man?

PAUL LYNDE: An unmarried young mother.

20. Who is more likely to fall out of a hospital bed: a man or a woman?

CHARLEY WEAVER: Out to the home, it usually happens simultaneously.

21. Anthropologist Margaret Mead writes, "It is a unique potential in women, the ability to . . ." To what?

PAUL LYNDE: Fake it.

22. If a man likes full-busted women, psychiatrists say he's likely to be ambitious. What can they tell about him if he goes for long-legged women?

ROSE MARIE: He's ambitious *and tall*.

23. According to recent studies at Stanford, is there anything inside a woman's body that makes her tend to cry more than men?

PAUL LYNDE: Yes, triplets!

24. You've been having trouble getting to sleep. Are you probably a man or a woman?

DON KNOTTS: That's what's keepin' me awake.

25. Within 5 percent, how many skydivers are women?

    JAN MURRAY: Before or after they hit the ground?

26. According to Karen Valentine's advice column, Ask Karen, there are two ways for a really skinny girl not to be mistaken for a boy. One is to wear your hair in a very feminine style. What's the other?

    PAUL LYNDE: Nurse in public.

27. A mermaid is half girl and half fish. What do you call a man who is half boy and half fish?

    CHARLEY WEAVER: Lonely.

28. Were cigar store "wooden indians" ever women?

    PAUL LYNDE: Only those made by a nervous whittler.

29. Royally speaking, how does a woman get to be the Queen Mother?

    MARTY ALLEN: Fool around with a king.

30. You're dreaming about a house. Are you more likely to be a man or a woman?

    CHARLEY WEAVER: What kind of house is it?

19. DOWN ON THE FARM

1. What should you call a female sheep?

   PAUL LYNDE: Beloved.

2. If a jackass and a mare fall in love, what will they pro-
   duce?

   MEL BROOKS: "The Dating Game."

3. What are "dual-purpose cattle" good for that other cattle
   aren't?

   PAUL LYNDE: They give milk . . . and cookies, but I
   don't recommend the cookies.

4. Chickens in a particular part of the country turn out more eggs per hen than anywhere else in the country. What state are they in?

   CHARLEY WEAVER: In almost constant pain.

5. Does your average rabbit mind being lifted up by his ears?

   PAUL LYNDE: During the mating season he considers it a favor.

6. What does a lamb have to do to become a sheep?

   ROSE MARIE: Be nice to the shepherd.

7. Before a cow will give you any milk, she has to have something very important. What?

   PAUL LYNDE: An engagement ring.

8. When it comes to baby chickens, is it pretty easy for the average person to tell the boys from the girls?

   JAN MURRAY: Take a peek while you're plucking!

9. We get wool from a sheep, but we get something special from an angora goat. What is it?

   PAUL LYNDE: Respect.

10. Just before he starts milking, there's one thing a good farmer does. What?

    CHARLEY WEAVER: Makes sure it's a cow.

11. Other than his crook or staff, what else did a shepherd have to protect him and his sheep?

    PAUL LYNDE: The Pill.

12. When does a cowboy call a horse a bronco?

    CHARLEY WEAVER: When they're alone together.

13. If a fox steals into your chicken coop one evening, the eggs the chickens lay for the next few days will probably be different than usual. What will be different about them?

PAUL LYNDE: They'll have long, bushy tails.

14. According to experts, male turkeys change something of theirs from blue to red when they want to attract a female turkey. What do they change?

JAN MURRAY: The light bulb in the coop.

15. It's sometimes called "the poor man's cow." What is it?

PAUL LYNDE: Bagpipes.

16. What do you call a pig that weighs more than 150 pounds?

CHARLEY WEAVER: A divorcee.

17. Right after Trigger died, what did Roy Rogers announce he would do?

PAUL LYNDE: Dismount.

18. Humans are identified by fingerprints. How can you tell cows apart?

CHARLEY WEAVER: Some udder way.

19. Are you apt to have much success if you try to cross a turkey with a chicken?

PAUL LYNDE: According to most chickens, it's a wonderful way to go.

20. The raccoon does something before he eats that few other animals do. What?

JIM BROLIN: He has a cocktail.

21. True or false: The Duke University Goat-watching Society recently did a long study and determined that, comparatively, goats are "delightful companions" for humans.

PAUL LYNDE: Yes, and I'd like to make an announcement.

22. According to experts, will you ever find a goose 29 thousand feet in the air?

CHARLEY WEAVER: Maybe in a very crowded 747 . . . in economy class.

23. Your horse has 40 teeth. Is it a boy horse or a girl horse?

PAUL LYNDE: Is that where you look?

24. Can guinea pigs whistle?

PAUL LYNDE: Only when they come to a boil.

25. In Kenya what can you usually tell about a man who has lots and lots and lots and lots of goats?

CHARLEY WEAVER: That he never takes his slippers off around the house.

26. You are milking your cow once a day. According to the World Book, are you living up to her expectations?

PAUL LYNDE: I must be. She broke up with the bull.

27. According to scientists, frogs have trouble telling boys from girls. If a boy frog grabs another boy frog, how does he know he's made a mistake?

CHARLEY WEAVER: Who said it was a mistake?

28. Do female frogs croak?

PAUL LYNDE: If you hold their little heads under water . . .

29. True or false: Turtles actually don't find other turtles very attractive.

JAN MURRAY: Actually they're attracted to sheep, but the sheep are too fast for 'em.

20. STAR-STUDDED

1. According to Omar Sharif, good breeding is the thing he admires most in women. What comes second?

   PAUL LYNDE: Bad breeding.

2. According to *T.V. Movie Screen*, Burt Reynolds is quoted as saying, "Dinah's in top form. I have never known anyone to be so completely able to throw herself into a . . ." A what?

   PAUL LYNDE: A headboard.

3. For the very first time, Liz Taylor recently became something people often make jokes about. What did she become?

   JIM BROLIN: Polish.

4. Connie Stevens shares something she uses in her nightclub act with her ex-husband, Eddie Fisher. Eddie is now using it in his act. What is it?

PAUL LYNDE: A sequin pants suit.

5. Jill St. John has something flown in from New York every Monday, Tuesday, and Wednesday. She says, "I think this is a magnificently healthy way to start the day." What was she talking about?

JAN MURRAY: The New York Jets.

6. According to Cary Grant, which does he prefer: a double bed or a king-size bed?

ROSE MARIE: If only I could tell you for sure.

7. Eva Gabor says there's a word she dislikes very much because it always signals the end of something that started out so beautifully. What word is it?

PAUL LYNDE: Pregnant.

8. Mae West recently stated that she not only bathes in it but she also drinks it. What is it?

CHARLEY WEAVER: Bath water.

9. According to Joyce Haber, there is one thing that Rock Hudson has never been able to think of himself as. What is it?

JAN MURRAY: A debutante.

10. Sophia Loren recently stated, "My Oscar meant nothing in Naples because acting means nothing. The one thing that is respected in Naples is . . ." What?

PAUL LYNDE: An elderly streetwalker.

11. Mickey Rooney was the first actor to do something with Esther Williams in a movie. Do what?

MARTY ALLEN: The breast stroke.

12. According to Elvis Presley, he got one four years ago, but one of his goals in life is that he'd like another one. Another what?

KAREN VALENTINE: Another hickey.

13. Lana Turner recently stated that she has been offered as much as a quarter of a million dollars to do something, but she won't do it. What?

PAUL LYNDE: Close her drapes.

14. After a 3-hour-and-15-minute battle, Frankie Laine recently got himself one that weighed 310 pounds. Just what did Frankie get himself?

JAN MURRAY: A hernia.

15. A highlight of an American star's recent Australian tour was the star's exhibition of baton-twirling while wearing red, white, and blue sequined hot pants and a decorated fringed jacket. Who was the star?

PAUL LYNDE: Vincent Price.

16. Patty Duke recently claimed that she has mastered 56 different ways of making something. What?

CHARLEY WEAVER: Whoopee.

17. According to Zsa Zsa Gabor, there is only one time when you really get to know a man. When is that?

LILY TOMLIN: Just before breakfast.

18. Robert Young recently stated, "I never, never give . . ." Something to his fans who ask for it. What?

PAUL LYNDE: A hysterectomy.

19. Dean Martin has been known to walk up eight flights of stairs rather than do something he hates to do. What?

PAUL LYNDE: Sleep alone.

20. Marlo Thomas is often asked by young girls, "How do I become an actress?" Marlo always tells them to get something first. Get what?

JAN MURRAY: Undressed.

21. James Stewart did it over 20 years ago when he was 41 years old. Now he says it was "one of the best things I ever did." What was it?

MARTY ALLEN: Rhonda Fleming.

22. Jane Fonda calls it the most beautiful thing in the world, as well as the most painful. What is it?

PAUL LYNDE: A sequinned whip.

23. Jackie Gleason recently revealed that he firmly believes in them and has actually seen them on at least two occasions. What are they?

CHARLEY WEAVER: His feet.

24. According to Robert Mitchum, one thing has ruined more actors than drinking. What?

CHARLEY WEAVER: Not drinking.

25. Ava Gardner says she can't really remember enjoying it, and only does it to get over her shyness. What was she talking about?

PAUL LYNDE: Makin' love.

26. Beatle John Lennon recently published his favorite photo of himself. It shows him smiling and sitting on top of something. What?

STU GILLIAM: Yoko Ono.

27. According to Marlene Dietrich, whenever she gives an interview, there is one question she is asked over and over. What is it?

PAUL LYNDE: "How about it, baby?"

28. Roy Rogers hasn't done it in 20 years, but there's speculation he may do it again soon. Do what?

CHARLEY WEAVER: Reupholster Trigger.

29. Anthony Quinn thinks they should be abolished, but he wouldn't turn one down. What are they?

PAUL LYNDE: Fifty-year-old women.

30. When Frank Sinatra made his great comeback performance in Las Vegas recently, he missed his second scheduled performance because something "just didn't feel right." What?

MARTY ALLEN: His slacks.

21. HISTORY

1. Before Columbus sailed to America, he made something for a living. What did he make?

   PAUL LYNDE: Passionate love to Queen Isabella.

2. In 1769, Daniel Boone started exploring something which he later described as a "terrestial paradise." What was he exploring?

   CHARLEY WEAVER: Dolly Madison.

3. According to the *Encyclopedia Brittanica*, Christopher Columbus first brought the seeds of something to the Western World. Then they began popping up in Florida,

then South America, and now they are all over California. What are they?

PAUL LYNDE: Bambinos.

4. Admiral Farragut is famous for his statement "Damn the torpedoes . . . full speed ahead!" Where was he when he said it?

CHARLEY WEAVER: In the tub.

5. According to the World Book, Francisco Pizarro became famous for his conquest of something. What?

PAUL LYNDE: Cesar Romero.

6. Only 40 men in the history of the United States can claim to have done it. One of them was Benjamin Franklin. Do what?

CHARLEY WEAVER: Put a smile on the face of Mrs. Franklin.

7. Alexander Graham Bell spoke the first words over the telephone. He said, "Watson, come here, I want you." Why did he want him?

JIM BROLIN: Just one of those crazy urges.

8. George Washington Carver was the man who was able to do 300 different things with . . . what?

PAUL LYNDE: Ruby Begonia.

9. True or false: In 1890, the U.S. issued a $5 bill which pictured Miss Liberty "topless" and holding a light bulb in her hand.

CHARLEY WEAVER: I didn't notice a light bulb.

10. Thomas Edison was a famous advocate of doing something every afternoon that he said helped get him through the day. What was it?

PAUL LYNDE: Madame Curie.

11. In 1931, two men in Russia slapped each other in the face continually for 300 hours. Why?

MARTY ALLEN: Just a lover's quarrel.

12. Napoleon offered a handsome prize to anyone who could come up with a cheap and wholesome substitute for it. For what?

PAUL LYNDE: Josephine.

13. In 1959, man got his first glimpse of the backside of something. What?

CHARLEY WEAVER: Was that the year Kate Smith fell down on the Ed Sullivan Show?

14. It was perfected in 1873 by a Major Walter Clopton Wingfield as a diversion for English society. What is it?

PAUL LYNDE: The vibrating crumpet.

15. When Russia's Nikita Khruschev visited this country in the late 50s, he was quite upset when he was told that he wouldn't be allowed to visit a famous place that has provided pleasure for millions. What was it?

ROSE MARIE: Frank Sinatra's bedroom.

16. A famous world landmark has been under U.S. control since 1903 but will gradually be given back to the country in which it is found. What is it?

MARTY ALLEN: Zza Zza Gabor.

17. On December 17, 1903, one of the most significant events in modern history took place ... although it only lasted about 12 seconds. What was it?

CHARLEY WEAVER: My second honeymoon.

18. In London, you might visit the place where some of the wives of Henry VIII were beheaded, where the little princes were imprisoned, and where a fantastic sample of torture instruments are displayed. What is it called?

PAUL LYNDE: Noel Coward's place.

19. Emperor Hirohito has been the Emperor of Japan for many years. Does he have an empress?

CHARLEY WEAVER: Not so much anymore.

20. In 1848, something was made for the first time, in Bangor, Maine, that millions of people have loved ever since. What?

PAUL LYNDE: Virginia Graham.

21. Benjamin Franklin kept four beds in his house, and he would switch from one to another whenever he felt something. Felt what?

CHARLEY WEAVER: Lonely.

22. ANIMAL WORLD

1. Should you be gentle when trying to awaken an elephant?

   PAUL LYNDE: I just leave peanuts on the dresser and tip-toe out.

2. Smokey the Bear has something written on his hat. What is it?

   LILY TOMLIN: "I'll never forget you," signed Ranger Roy.

3. We all know Smokey the Bear's motto: "Only *you* can prevent forest fires," but what exactly is the request that Woodsy Owl makes of us?

   PAUL LYNDE: "Keep that dirty bear away from me."

4. According to *Cosmopolitan's Love Guide,* is it a good sign if your man loves animals?

   JOAN RIVERS: Not to excess.

5. According to author Desmond Morris, do chimpanzees kiss exactly the same way humans do?

   PAUL LYNDE: (wink) Better!

6. You see a reindeer charging at you, and you notice that it has antlers. Can you be certain that it's a male?

   ROSE MARIE: I'll take my chances and just freshen up.

7. You're in the woods with a friend and a snake bites him. What's the first thing you should do?

   PAUL LYNDE: Find a new friend.

8. There are three reasons we know of why a male lion roars. One is that he is angry, another is he is hungry. What is the third?

   CHARLEY WEAVER: His shorts are too tight.

9. You have an uncontrollable urge to kill a walrus. The authorities won't let you, though, unless you can prove that you are a . . . what?

   PAUL LYNDE: A jealous husband.

10. Blue, gray, and humpback are all kinds of something. Kinds of what?

    KAREN VALENTINE: Colors.

11. There is only one living thing that the average polar bear is afraid of. What?

    PAUL LYNDE: A lonely Eskimo.

12. True or false: If a grizzly bear breaks into your camp, the first thing he'll probably go for is your sweets.

    CHARLEY WEAVER: Yes, so be sure and lock her in your sleeping bag.

13. A little bear is called a cub. A little cow is a calf. What should you call a little goose?

    PAUL LYNDE: Annoying.

14. Does the average elephant feel more romantic in a zoo or in the wild?

    ROSE MARIE: I haven't found much difference, Pete.

15. Rubbing an alligator's stomach has a curious effect on him. What does rubbing his tummy make him do?

    PAUL LYNDE: Eat you.

16. We all know that your little house cat can purr when it's happy. But is there anything that will make a big wild tiger purr?

    ROSE MARIE: Probably your little house cat.

17. You are wandering through the jungle when you suddenly come upon a large group of baboons, who immediately start smacking their lips and grunting softly. What are they trying to tell you?

    PAUL LYNDE: They *want* me.

18. You have just scolded your gorilla for being a bad boy. Might he stick out his tongue at you to show his anger?

   PAUL LYNDE: Was that his tongue?

19. Do gorillas have a high sex drive?

   CHARLEY WEAVER: No, but they like to monkey around.

23. MUSIC AND SONG

1. According to the classic song, "millions of hearts have been broken just because these words were spoken." What words?

PAUL LYNDE: "I'm going to have your baby."

2. According to the song, "When we are dancing and you're dangerously near me," what happens?

CHARLEY WEAVER: Well, out to the home if anything happens they write it up in the medical journal.

3. According to the old alphabet song, "A, you're adorable: "B, you're so beautiful: "C, you're a cutie full of charms. When you're a D, what are you?

PAUL LYNDE: Top-heavy.

4. According to the lyrics of a well-known song, "I've got rhythm, and I've got music." What else do I have?

McLEAN STEVENSON: I've got six kids . . . and I *don't* have rhythm.

5. According to the old song, "I took one look at you, that's all I meant to do, and then" . . . something happened. What?

PAUL LYNDE: I fell off the fire escape (I was peekin').

6. In the old standard, "South of the Border," "I fell in love down Mexico way" when something came out. When what came out?

CHARLEY WEAVER: Thursday's lunch.

7. The song "Where Do I Begin?" is the theme song for what hit movie?

PAUL LYNDE: *Bob & Carol & Ted & Alice.*

8. There's a gospel hymn that says, "It was good enough for father, it's good enough for me." What is it?

CHARLEY WEAVER: That's Mrs. Ferguson out to the home.

9. According to the old song, "A Bicycle Built for Two," why am I half crazy?

PAUL LYNDE: (in pain) My seat's too high.

10. According to *Candid Viewer* Magazine, sometimes when Fred MacMurray wants to relax, he uses something he once used in a band but admits that it "sounds pretty bad." What is it?

REDD FOXX: Helen O'Connell.

11. In music, you put together two violinists, one cellist, and one player of a viola . . . and what do you have?

PAUL LYNDE: A crush on the cellist.

12. What famous singer once said that a great singer needed a big mouth, 90 percent memory, 10 percent intelligence, lots of hard work, something in the heart, and a big chest?

CHARLEY WEAVER: Eddie Fisher, and then somebody stole his big chest!

13. According to the American Music Conference, two musical instruments that we usually associate with men are becoming increasingly popular with women. One of them is the drums. What's the other?

PAUL LYNDE: I know an accordian gives 'em a thrill.

14. According to music experts, is the piano the best thing for you to train your young child on?

CHARLEY WEAVER: No, try newspapers.

15. What do you call that musical instrument that's shaped like a triangle?

PAUL LYNDE: Connie Stevens.

16. According to *Coronet* Magazine, is it a good idea to play music when you make love?

CHARLEY WEAVER: Not if you play the tuba.

17. In music who was responsible for St. Matthew's Passion?

PAUL LYNDE: St. Theresa.

24. SPORTS, GAMES, HOBBIES

1. According to *Family Weekly*, the most popular hobby in America is photography. What comes next?

   PAUL LYNDE: Blackmail.

2. In bowling, what's a perfect score?

   ROSE MARIE: Ralph, the pin boy!

3. If you're going to make a parachute jump, you should be at least how high?

   CHARLEY WEAVER: Three days of steady drinking should do it.

4. In 1953, the world's greatest weight lifter, Paul Anderson, lifted 6,000 pounds. What did he get for it?

   PAUL LYNDE: The world's biggest hernia.

5. Where would you find a jockey's silks?

   JIM BROLIN: Under his evening gown.

6. In what sport could you win a prize for the best "abdominals"?

   PAUL LYNDE: Celebrity childbirth.

7. Ginger Rogers once attributed her 19-inch waistline to a certain sport. What sport?

   MARTY ALLEN: Fred Astaire.

8. If you said, "I am a funny little dutch girl, as funny as can be, and all the boys around my block are crazy over me," what would you be doing while you said it?

   CHARLEY WEAVER: Trying to stay out of the Army.

9. If you won the Mexican open, what kind of athlete would you be?

   PAUL LYNDE: A runner!

10. Robin Hood entered Prince John's archery contest and got a kiss from Maid Marion. What was first prize in the contest?

    MARTY ALLEN: A kiss from Prince John.

11. James Ellis and Joseph Frazier recently held it together, and Mr. Frazier is currently holding it alone. What is it?

    JAN MURRAY: Mrs. Frazier.

12. Mainly, when he's deep under the ocean, two things are sent through the diver's hose. Oxygen is one. What's the other?

PAUL LYNDE: The 23rd psalm.

13. According to *Time* Magazine, what is the sport on which Americans spend the most money?

HARVEY KORMAN: Adultery.

14. A Russian named Petrosian recently used the Sicilian Defense and lost. Lost what?

PAUL LYNDE: His deep voice.

15. What is the most popular participant sport in nudist camps?

ROSE MARIE: Button, Button, Who's Got the Button?

16. The most important rule of scuba diving is: "Never dive without . . ." Without what?

PAUL LYNDE: Your trunks.

17. In professional boxing, can you lose a fight for hitting your opponent below the belt?

MARTY ALLEN: Yes, but that's nothing compared to his problem.

18. Technically, in baseball, what do you call the area between the batter's knees and his armpits?

PAUL LYNDE: The erogenous zone.

19. At a wrestling match, how does someone score?

    JIM BACKUS: Same as anywhere: make friends and offer to buy her a drink.

20. Famed basketball star Wilt Chamberlain says that he keeps in shape during the off season by doing something he really enjoys. What is it?

    JAN MURRAY: Peering into fourth-floor windows.

21. Your wife has just won the Uber Cup. What did she have to do to get it?

    PAUL LYNDE: Ask Uber.

22. William Moore, America's oldest living professional athlete, has just retired at age 100. What is his sport?

    CHARLEY WEAVER: The prune toss.

23. For a long time now, daredevil motorcycle rider Evil Knievel has wanted to jump over something, but the Government won't let him. What is it?

    SALLY STRUTHERS: Julie Nixon Eisenhower.

24. Before athletic competition, ancient Greek athletes covered their body with something. What?

    MARTY ALLEN: Rita, the Goddess of Conquest.

25. Is bowling big in Japan?

    LILY TOMLIN: *Nothing* is big in Japan.

26. What is a female bullfighter called in Mexico?

    CHARLEY WEAVER: Before the last fight, she was called José Garcia.

25. AROUND THE WORLD

1. In ancient Egypt, every able-bodied man was required to spend several months a year working on something. What?

   PAUL LYNDE: Cleopatra.

2. True or false: mountain climbers in Switzerland are complaining that the Matterhorn does not have enough bathroom facilities.

   CHARLEY WEAVER: Especially the climbers at the bottom.

3. Is whipping legal in Canada?

   PAUL LYNDE: Yes, and very popular.

4. What group of people is famous for ending a good hunt by tossing everybody in a blanket?

JOAN RIVERS: Movie producers.

5. In a guide for American businessman who are going to Russia, it tells them to do one particular thing immediately after having a glass of vodka. What should they do?

PAUL LYNDE: Grab a woman.

6. In Hawaiian, does it take more than three words to say "I love you"?

VINCENT PRICE: No. You can say it with a pineapple and a twenty.

7. In Morocco, if you see a man walk up to a young lady and break a raw egg on her forehead, you can be pretty sure that she is just about to do something. What is that?

PAUL LYNDE: Use her knee.

8. According to custom, where does an Austrian kiss a lady when he meets her?

JAN MURRAY: On the alps.

9. In France, boys don't whistle at attractive girls. What do they do to show their appreciation?

PAUL LYNDE: Rip off their clothes.

10. According to the National Environmental Research Center, in the summer, an Eskimo will frequently pay up to $5 for a big cake of ice. Because that provides him with . . . what?

MARTY ALLEN: Companionship.

11. What happens if you give a wolf-whistle to a woman in Cairo, Egypt?

    PAUL LYNDE: She'll tell her camel to soil you.

12. The Swedish Government gives women $256 every time they do something. What?

    CHARLEY WEAVER: I don't know, but they leave it on the dresser.

13. Overweight Germans have been asked to lay off the national dish. What is the national dish?

    JAN MURAY: Elke Sommer.

14. On New Year's Eve in Scotland, it's traditional to wish that a person will have a fire in his hearth, money in his purse, and something on his table. What?

    PAUL LYNDE: His secretary.

15. Traditionally, when a Britisher gets this job, he pretends to be reluctant and two of his co-workers grab him and drag him to his new seat. What is the job?

    MARTY ALLEN: Queen.

16. Japanese television has lured Audrey Hepburn out of retirement to model some common items that they feel only Audrey can do justice to. What is she modeling?

    PAUL LYNDE: Chop sticks.

17. Jackie Onassis once described it as a "bunch of men stamping around and yelling and going without a bath for three days." What was she referring to?

    PAUL LYNDE: A Greek honeymoon.

18. In the United States, how often must a commercial airline pilot get a physical check-up?

    JOAN RIVERS: Every 1200 hours . . . or new stewardess . . . whichever comes first.

19. You're on your first visit to Japan, and you head right for the Kabuki. Why?

    PAUL LYNDE: It was a long plane ride.

20. True or false: Some African Watusi tribesmen greet guests by running toward them at full pace, then high-jumping over them.

    CHARLEY WEAVER: This is sometimes terribly embarrassing to tall guests.

21. Where did the custom of kissing a lady's hand begin?

    PAUL LYNDE: At the shoulder.

22. In Denmark, if you looked up and saw a couple of storks on your roof, it would mean you were going to have something. What?

    CHARLEY WEAVER: Stork fazoo.

23. You are leaving Hawaii by boat. Now legend says you will return if you do something. What?

    PAUL LYNDE: Have Don Ho's baby.

24. According to research in London, what is considered to be the worst enemy of sleep?

    CHARLEY WEAVER: Beer.

26. MOVIES AND TV

1. In the 1930s, a Tarzan movie was made near Silver Springs, Florida, and when it was done, the film crews left something behind. Now these things are becoming a menace. What are they?

   PAUL LYNDE: About now they'd be teenagers!

2. In the classic *Wizard of Oz* the lion wanted courage and the tin man wanted a heart. What did the scarecrow want?

   CHARLEY WEAVER: A woman!

3. What popular T.V. show has a theme song called "You're Going to Make It After All"?

   JIM BACKUS: "Love, American Style."

4. When the Doris Day Show starts, Doris comes down a staircase, smiles a big smile, and then says three words which helped make her famous. What are these three words?

   PAUL LYNDE: "Don't touch me!"

5. Dennis Weaver, Debbie Reynolds, and Shelley Winters star in the movie *What's the Matter with Helen?* In the movie, who plays Helen?

   CHARLEY WEAVER: Dennis Weaver—that's why they ask the question.

6. What gave Mary Poppins the ability to fly?

   PAUL LYNDE: Somethin' she sniffed.

7. In the movie *One Million Years B.C.*, the two humans were Tumac and Loana. Tumac was of the Rock People. Raquel Welch played Loana. What people was she from?

   MARTY ALLEN: The Grapefruit People.

8. In *The Wizard of Oz*, the tin man wanted a heart and the scarecrow wanted a brain. What did the lion want?

   PAUL LYNDE: Dorothy.

9. Who did Dyan Cannon play in the movie *Bob & Carol & Ted & Alice*?

   JOAN RIVERS: Both Bob and Ted.

10. In a classic scene, Kirk Douglas and Burt Lancaster met for a shootout at a famous Western spot. Where did they meet?

    JIM BROLIN: At Jill St. John's.

11. In the movies, who gave the advice "whistle while you work"?

    PAUL LYNDE: It was either Linda Lovelace or Paul Winchell.

12. In the old Cisco Kid T.V. series, Pancho would smile at the Cisco Kid every week at the end of the show and say, "Oh, Cisco!" What did Cisco answer?

    CHARLEY WEAVER: "Let go of me, Pancho."

13. What is the familiar phrase that is repeated hundreds of times a year by the highest-paid female model on commercial television?

    MARTY ALLEN: "Is the door locked?"

14. According to the head NBC censor, when it comes to movies to be seen on T.V., the networks check for three things: violence, sex, and . . . and what else?

    PAUL LYNDE: Originality.

15. Lovely Karen Valentine made her film debut in a movie called *Gidget . . . Does something*. Gidget what?

    PAUL LYNDE: *Gidget Gets Morning Sickness*.

16. In the popular book and movie, *The Andromeda Strain,* what is the Andromeda Strain?

    JAN MURRAY: It's a Greek hernia.

17. On the old Roy Rogers Show, did Dale Evans wear a gun, too?

    CHARLEY WEAVER: Yes. They both did. And they had to be *very careful* when they hugged.

18. In the old Sergeant Preston television show, the good sergeant ended every spisode by saying something to his faithful dog. What did he say?

PAUL LYNDE: "I'll get the lights, dear."

19. At a recent Hollywood auction, something was sold which Liz Taylor used a lot in the movie *Cleopatra*. What was it?

JOAN RIVERS: Rex Harrison.

20. According to *Life* Magazine, Rock Hudson was recently with the eight girls who will appear with him in a new movie, and his comment was "Yechh." Why?

MARTY ALLEN: They were naked?

21. When the Lone Ranger was finished with a case, he left something behind. What?

PAUL LYNDE: A masked baby.

22. True or False: on a recent talk show, Joey Heatherton said, "I am *not* a sexpot."

JAN MURRAY: She's right, Pete, but you're a damn good M.C.

"Quote—Unquote"

1. "A little learning."
2. He's married.
3. Youth.
4. Getting what one wants.
5. "Rival."
6. Prosperity.
7. "Annabelle Lee". From the poem of the same name.
8. Africa.
9. Truth.
10. Danger.
11. Gloom of night.
12. "They are ours."
13. Poverty.
14. Ideas.
15. A cigarette.
16. Duty.
17. The devil, of course.
18. Same thing—"Be prepared."
19. Think.
20. Problems.

Body Language

1. "What about the pill?"
2. 5 percent.
3. True.
4. Take them out.
5. The mouth. They're teeth.
6. Gum damage.
7. Yes, it will, but a lip balm will work better.
8. Measles. Those are classic symptoms.
9. Kiss the blarney stone.
10. No. Chances are very slim.
11. False eyelashes, which Raquel feels add to any face.
12. The upper arm.
13. One that's too soft.
14. Sleep.
15. Above.
16. Near her eyes. Cilia are eyelashes.

17. No, one inch less.
18. Uncooperative.
19. It's an old wives' tale.
20. Yes. In fact, there's a park ranger in Virginia who holds the record. He's been struck five times.
21. True.
22. Tonsils.
23. The lotus position.
24. Insomnia.
25. No. It would be nice for a change.
26. No. It can break off the hair and cause tangles, but it doesn't cause permanent damage.
27. Young folks.
28. Your bladder.
29. House calls. They are most costly and often less efficient.
30. A phobia. That's the definition of phobia.
31. No. It has the opposite effect of killing hair growth.
32. Yes.
33. Housewife. The doctor thinks it's more important than any other occupation or profession.
34. He performed a heart transplant.
35. Poor posture—according to *Today's Health* Magazine.
36. You might be on the sunny side of the bus for hours.
37. Exercise.
38. Yes. And *Playboy* uses the information for their magazine articles.
39. True. And most will only treat married couples.
40. True. They say its healthier that way.
41. "Do you take the pill?"
42. Five.
43. True—according to the American Society for Bariatircs.
44. True.
45. About three pounds.
46. The sun.
47. Smaller.
48. A facial masque.
49. Sleeping with someone else.
50. No, probably not. The medulla oblongata is part of the brain.
51. Yes.
52. Yes.
53. Liquids. Nothing by mouth until the doctor's okay.
54. It's down while you are sleeping.
55. Vanity.
56. You should give your eyes a chance to adjust to the darkness, according to the National Safety Council.
57. No need to make a production of it. The "excuse me" will only attract more attention than you should want.
58. His hand. He had muscle spasms that closed his hand into a fist.

59. Shivering. The first natural response is goose pimples.
60. Cold cream.
61. No. Bow legs and knock knees correct themselves.
62. Wear slack suits instead of dresses.
63. True.

Legend and Literature

1. An apple.
2. A tree, too. He was an ash and she was an elm.
3. Make you dream.
4. Snakes. He strangled them.
5. A tree.
6. Oranges.
7. Sew.
8. Vultures.
9. From wearing a poisoned shirt.
10. His daughter.
11. Crazy. But finally he had to go anyway.
12. False. Diana was.
13. A tree.
14. He fulfilled the prophecy and became a great ruler.
15. The unicorn, which is why virgins were needed to capture unicorns.
16. He was a tailor.
17. Johnny Appleseed.
18. A piece of the wedding cake.
19. Magic. He'll have magical powers.
20. It means you'll soon marry.
21. A pillar of salt.
22. Yes.
23. The Garden of Eden.
24. An angel.
25. By letting his hair grow long again.
26. Modesty.
27. Marriage—to Romeo—whom she had just met.
28. "A Midsummer Night's Dream" by Shakespeare.
29. Shakespeare's "Othello."

Junior and Senior Citizens

1. Yes, according to a recent U.S.C. study. But one has yet to discover what they dream *about*.
2. 6 months.
3. No.
4. True.

5. True. By an 80 percent chance.
6. Throw a tantrum. This is the most common reaction.
7. Thumb suckers.
8. No. The child may sense your discomfort and that may influence him to regard the subject as unhealthy.
9. Let him have something else. The dinner table should not be a a battle ground.
10. No. It's harmless.
11. Yes. A roller-skating merit badge.
12. A good turn, helping someone.
13. Yes.
14. Yes.
15 "Where do babies come from?"
16. No. Let him sleep through and he'll probably forget the whole thing by morning.
17. No. It's considered perfectly normal in the early years of a child's life.
18. Take the food away and dismiss him from the table.
19. No, not at all. Nature will obey the laws of supply and demand.
20. Yes, always.
21. The father.
22. Miss Frances.
23. Your sense of smell.
24. Yes. Elderly people are more likely to choke.
25. Companionship, of course.
26. False. They need less and less.
27. No.
28. Heredity. Her family background.
29. A house.
30. No. More power to him.
21. Vitamin Q.
32. Married.
33. Yes. Hormone injections might help.
34. Sex.
35. He says no.

Pregnancy and The Pill

1. Yes, assuming she is otherwise healthy.
2. Yes. Outgoing, extroverted.
3. True.
4. True. The punishment is postponed.
5. Because of her career.
6. Yes, it happens.
7. Elephants carry their babies for 22 months.
8. True. 1957 was the all-time banner year for births.

9. The woman who takes the pill, according to studies in London.
10. Yes.
11. Smoke.
12. Yes. Have a check-up.
13. If you are pregnant.
14. A boy. But it's just an old wives' tale.
15. True. Research is being done on a certain kind of orchid seed.
16. Yes. Pregnant women should never use pesticides.
17. Yes.
18. Keep you from having babies. It's like the Pill but with less side effects.
19. The baby does—usually 120 beats per minute.
20. Yes.
21. True. The moon may be affecting our biological cycles.

The Birds and The Bees, Etc.

1. Remove the stinger.
2. Because they are so stupid.
3. Dying. Most die fairly soon.
4. The snail. It takes three weeks to cover one mile.
5. False.
6. A locust.
7. Keep it covered.
8. Twice a year.
9. By following her flashing lights.
10. She releases a scent.
11. See.
12. Probably a boy, since most girl canaries don't sing.
13. To get them interested in making honey. Bees are sometimes slow to get to work in the spring.
14. For eating. They are considered a rare delicacy.
15. To lead them or treat them if they are ill. The sock prevents them from becoming frightened.
16. By a mule. The ostrich can kick much harder.

LSD—Love, Sex, and Dating

1. "Let's leave."
2. Preferably at a public place, like a restaurant, because you might weaken alone at night.
3. Tell him to cut it out. If that doesn't work, get rid of him.
4. Play tennis.
5. When she's wearing gloves.
6. No, according to *Glamour* Magazine.
7. A princess—Princess Soraya.

8. Great friends.
9. Football.
10. Yes.
11. No. If he hasn't said so, chances are he wouldn't be sincere in following her hint.
12. Outdoors.
13. Horses.
14. Acting.
15. False.
16. No.
17. "Will you marry me?"
18. Liberated.
19. 6 months.
20. Yes.
21. 6 months. Any longer makes a risky marriage.
22. A chaperone—very proper for Spanish girls.
23. Eyes.
24. His mother.
25. Crying.
26. Yes. Get more experience. This may calm you down or you may need psychological counseling.
27. "Where do you want to go?"

Newsmakers

1. Important.
2. Teaching school.
3. He's Surgeon General of the United States.
4. Married.
5. A tape.
6. Marriage and family life.
7. "Square."
8. In the State Department.
9. She made her film debut.
10. Just as the wife of a President.
11. Housewife.
12. "Ouch."
13. Herself. She holds long conversations with herself.
14. "Tell a shady joke," an off-color story.
15. Chefs.
16. The right to vote.
17. In South America.
18. Ride a horse.
19. True.
20. A poodle.
21. Speak at Republican rallies.
22. Karate. "Providence has been very good to the people who haven't tested me," he says.
23. A sense of humor.

Books, Stories, and Comics

1. Poetry, to his wife.
2. Joan. The author is Joan Garrity.
3. It's a cookbook.
4. The sea.
5. Encounter groups and other therapy involving the touching and hugging of other people.
6. The sun.
7. *Little Men.*
8. Ernest Hemingway.
9. Love.
10. Royal Navy.
11. His sore toe.
12. She hates them, that's why.
13. The trauma of birth.
14. The brain.
15. Spying. Lucy was a famous spy in World War II.
16. *The $2,000,000 Honeymoon.*
17. "Unscared," or relaxed.
18. True.
19. "Ain't." Everybody hates it.
20. 200.
21. "Can."
22. On his spurs.
23. Checkers, their late, great dog.
24. Phone numbers. In Moscow you have to buy their phone book.
25. Croquet.
26. *1984* by George Orwell.
27. You should fall asleep. That's what the treatment is for.
28. Bacteria—germs.
29. It frightened a mouse.
30. The white rabbit.
31. The little engine that could.
32. To have a child. And she eventually had sleeping beauty.
33. Rabbit skin.
34. The word "Christmas."
35. Heidi.
36. Anything yellow.
37. A golden thunderbolt.
38. Long hair, sideburns, and new glasses.

Sex, Education, and Violence

1. Pretend you're still asleep. Don't startle him. Call the police as soon as he leaves.
2. That his wife will go out and find someone better than he is.

3. True.
4. Anger.
5. True. It's a 16-minute short on venereal disease.
6. No. The overwelming majority go unreported.
7. Power.
8. Other children, according to a *Good Housekeeping* poll.
9. Learning from one's parents. Particularly by observing a wholesome give-and-take relationship in the home.
10. Yes. To reassure himself of his masculinity.
11. No. It's a no-no.
12. Yes. Definitely
13. Give him your money, or, as they put it, "Give up, shut up, and pay up."
14. The bedroom.
15. No, you should simply hang up.
16. Take them off so that you can use them as a weapon if necessary.
17. Yes, they are.
18. Saturday night—8 P.M. to 2 A.M.
19. Scream.
20. In the Adam's apple The throat.
21. Postal inspector.
22. Turn and go in the opposite direction. Then he will be forced to turn around to follow you. You do it again, etc.
23. Drop it in the nearest mailbox. (It can be reclaimed from the Post Office by describing its contents.)
24. "I'll give you whatever you want."
25. Yes, as loud as you can.
26. In marriage.
27. "Fire." This gets more attention than just "help."

Marriage

1. 9 out of 10 said yes.
2. Love.
3. The heart, of course.
4. Yes, by 2 to 1.
5. Yes.
6. Honesty.
7. Yes. There are enough surprises in marriages without adding this one.
8. A wedding cake.
9. The mother of the bride. It's the signal to start.
10. "Are you a friend of the bride or the groom?"
11. A lucky six-pence.
12. A civil marriage.
13. The minister's fee.

14. No.
15. Yes.
16. 24.
17. Wheat.
18. Cows.
19. Kissed.
20. No. Try to find out in a more subtle way.
21. 27.
22. No. Veils are for first times.
23. No. For most couples it takes longer than that.
24. A son.
25. Yes.
26. Yes.
27. Her maiden name.
28. Money.
29. True.
30. Break the stems of the glasses.
31. How many children they should have.
32. Yes. It can save you time and money.
33. The couple in their twenties.
34. The hubby.
35. True.
36. Your wife. Birds have almost no sense of taste.
37. The guest.
38. Government.
39. Yes, it's perfectly proper.
40. Inhibitions.
41. No. A woman need not appear in lobby to register.
42. False. There's no such law.
43. To have children.
44. No. Height plays no important part.
45. 40.
46. Why he's lost interest in her.
47. "I'm sorry."
48. Taller.
49. Bigamy.
50. Most adults are married.
51. Watching T.V.
52. No, it's very normal.
53. Yes.
54. At golf.
55. True.
56. Get a divorce. If your marriage is that bad, there's no hope.
57. Yes. She can take him to court to collect.
58. Yes. What is good for the children is not always good for the marriage.
59. Money problems.
60. Yes. To the eighth Mrs. Rooney.
61. Money.

62. Food.
63. Stockings.
64. Loneliness. It's hard to really prepare yourself for being alone today.
65. Alimony.
66. True.
67. Singing.
68. The wife.
69. Yes. Be nice, says Abby.
70. Divorced men.
71. Jealousy. Money is number two, and cards are number three.
72. "I divorce you" or "I divorce thee."
73. Find someone else.
74. True.
75. True. Plastic or paper.
76. Something made of gold.
77. "Bad news."

Facts and Figures

1. Yes.
2. True.
3. True.
4. No, just a limit on the number of pieces.
5. Centrifugal force.
6. "Taps."
7. The speed of light.
8. True.
9. The G.I. Bill of Rights.
10. True. From smoking in bed.
11. Yes. Supine means you're lying on your back.
12. A liquid.
13. Snoring. You're more apt to snore while you're sleeping on your back.
14. 5 minutes. Any longer and you're probably doing it wrong.
15. The closet. The small room will probably give you more protection.
16. True. It's a new rule.
17. Yes. It's called a nano-second.
18. True.
19. Yes, if you provide more than half of her total support.
20. True.
21. 5'1".
22. Earthquakes.
23. They developed shorthand.
24. Yes.
25. Lie down flat with your arms outstretched. You will float, according to the World Book.

26. True.
27. True. Anything made from an endangered species of animal is now illegal to sell in New York.
28. True.
29. Tickling.
30. Every six years.

Man's Best Friends

1. Yes. According to experts, dogs can suffer from the same emotional problems as people.
2. Yes. A dog's eyesight has been known to improve with glasses.
3. Yes. There's always a chance of picking up some infection.
4. Yes.
5. A Siamese.
6. No. Dogs eat grass to prevent not feeling well.
7. True.
8. He is ready for breeding.
9. Stretch.
10. No, they just went along as mascots.

Name Dropping

1. Write a book.
2. Flip Wilson. Referring to Geraldine, of course.
3. His yacht.
4. True.
5. "Wunnerful."
6. His mind.
7. He couldn't pronounce her name.
8. 35.
9. The 69-carat diamond.
10. False.
11. Yes.
12. Riding.
13. Her hubby, Richard.
14. A bed.
15. Kiss.
16. Wealth, or money. It spoils them.
17. Uncomfortable.
18. False.
19. Entertainment.
20. Intelligent.
21. In "The Fugitive."
22. A Christmas tree.
23. About 9 A.M. He stays up all night.

24. Health spas.
25. A daughter.
26. A role in one of his spectaculars.
27. No.
28. That they're getting a divorce.
29. A chair.
30. "Woman."
31. Accordian.
32. The Hawaiian language.
33. Work.

Dressed or Undressed

1. The vast majority said no.
2. Hercules. It was one of his twelve labors.
3. No, it's quite common.
4. Yes.
5. Varicose veins.
6. Yes.
7. It impedes circulation.
8. True.
9. Two years.
10. Baldness.
11. 97 percent said no.
12. Smile. Clerks will stay away from those who are scowling.
13. Yes.
14. Yes, and most have children.
15. Religion.
16. True.
17. Recreation.
18. No.
19. Shoes.
20. True.
21. Her size. She's small and feels loud clothes will make her more noticeable.
22. Dress designing.
23. Glasses.
24. No. She's against them.
25. His pants. The chaps are leather covers.
26. Just above.
27. Rinse it in cold water to remove chlorine and/or salt.
28. False. Skin oils are bad for the fur.
29. No.

1. True.
2. The apple.
3. Of the wines, which wine to try.
4. Yes. They're a big favorite.
5. Live forever.
6. May. Strawberries are at their best.
7. Bananas.
8. California.
9. Yes. It's suggested it makes them taste better.
10. There's a shortage.
11. Yes. They loved pears and even painted pictures of them in theiir tombs.
12. False.
13. Yes. Prunes are rich in vitamins and can give your blood a boost.
14. Butter.
15. Your brain.
16. Because you'll get about twice as much juice.
17. Smell it, of course.
18. Each course at a different home or restaurant.
19. A half teaspoon.
20. True. Otherwise you can waste wine and bubbles.
21. Yes, you can.
22. Yes. A yogurt facial mask is good for the skin, according to *Women's Wear Daily*.
23. A creamery.
24. The bones.
25. No. It's a bad idea for health reasons.
26. Remove the bones.
27. Yes, about 65 calories in an average serving.
28. Yes. Prunes are a common stuffing for goose.
29. Yes.
30. It's fresh and good to buy.
31. She was trying to improve her complexion. It was a facial treatment.
32. Bacon.
33. Dry it in the sun.
34. True.
35. Jewelry.
36. Irish coffee.
37. She feeds them her own cooking.
38. Yes. She's an excellent cook and has written a cookbook.
39. Drink it. It's a popular wine drink.
40. Bottled water.

Who, What and Where

1. Lawyers.
2. The kitchen.
3. His shoes, the famous wooden shoes of Holland.
4. Bleach—using it improperly or excessively.
5. A watch repairman.
6. The piano. "Two Girls at the Piano."
7. The Camp Fire Girls.
8. Queen Elizabeth of England.
9. Animal Skins.
10. The graveyard shift.
11. Sherlock Holmes.
12. Tents.
13. A college. They are the seven Ivy League women's colleges.
14. A faculty advisor.
15. A yacht. *The Christina.*
16. His chair.
17. Docking.
18. Chains.
19. A weekend pass.
20. The purser.
21. No. That word is only about ten years old.
22. The sapphire.
23. Eight cents.
24. A water bed.
25. CARE.
26. Curing the hiccups.
27. The steering wheel.
28. Yes. We had one in 1972 when one second was added.
29. Gymnasium.
30. A volcano eruption—Krakatoa in 1883. It was heard 2,500 miles away.
31. Golden Gate Bridge, Hoover Dam, Mount Rushmore, Statue of Liberty, Disney World, Gateway Arch, Houston Astrodome.
32. A hotel.
33. Breakfast.
34. Silverware.
35. Irreplaceable.
36. In Hawaii. A spot there gets 451 inches of rain a year.
37. Carpenter (builder).
38. Red hair.
39. Expo '70. They had 64 million visitors in 6 months.
40. Their names.
41. Lady jockeys.
42. A merman.
43. Unlisted telephone numbers.
44. Eggs.

45. Volcanos.
46. A nickle.
47. In London's subway.

Male or Female

1. Women discuss men about three times more than men discuss women.
2. Yes, according to an Australian psychologist. A woman's snore invariably ends in a wheeze.
3. No. Women sit on the edge and swing their legs up, while men get in feet first.
4. True.
5. The girl—just the way its always been.
6. "Brava."
7. Lose excess weight.
8. She says she's married to one.
9. Honesty.
10. $3.
11. An abbot.
12. True, according to the border patrol.
13. Diamonds.
14. They were very rude.
15. Yes, an overwhelming majority do.
16. The low pay.
17. The woman. They have far more accidents on the average than men.
18. Yes, three of them.
19. His mother.
20. A man. For some reason, twice as many men as women.
21. Bear children.
22. He's very shy.
23. Yes. The female hormone estrogen seems to have an effect on crying.
24. You're a woman, according to the International Family Health Encyclopedia.
25. 20 percent.
26. Wear super-feminine clothes.
27. A merman.
28. Yes. In fact, 80 percent were—to attract more customers.
29. She's the king's widow, and her child is the reigning king or queen.
30. A woman, according to Dr. Joyce Brothers.

Down on The Farm

1. A ewe.
2. A mule.
3. They're good for both beef and milk production.
4. California.
5. Yes. Never lift him by his legs or ears because you'll injure him.
6. Celebrate its first birthday.
7. A calf.
8. No, it takes an expert.
9. Mohair.
10. He washes the cow's udder, for good sanitation.
11. His dog.
12. Before the horse had been broken or tamed.
13. The shells will be thicker.
14. Their necks. Their necks change color.
15. A goat.
16. A hog. (Also swine, boar, sow)
17. Have the horse stuffed.
18. Nose prints. Every cow's nose is unique.
19. Yes. You'll get a fowl known as a "turkhen."
20. He washes his food.
21. True.
22. Yes. They've been photographed that high.
23. A boy. Most males have 40 teeth, the females only 36.
24. His food. The gopher's favorite foods are roots.
25. He's wealthy.
26. No. Cows are milked twice a day.
27. The other one growls a special noise that, hopefully, all other frogs will honor.
28. No.
29. False.

Star Studded

1. Intelligence.
2. A game. Dinah is an avid tennis player.
3. A mother-in-law.
4. Connie's brother, who is a drummer.
5. Clams on the half shell. She has them for breakfast.
6 A double bed.
7. Alimony.
8. Bottled spring water.
9. Rock Hudson. He's never been able to get used to that name. He hates it.
10. Singing.

11. Kiss her. In her first film, *AndyHardy's Double life.*
12. Child. He has one daughter but would like another child.
13. Write her autobiography. "I haven't finished living my life by a long shot."
14. A fish. A swordfish, off Catalina Island.
15. Liberace.
16. Hamburger.
17. When you divorce him.
18. Medical advice. "I have to remind them that I'm only an actor."
19. Take the elevator. Dino hates elevators.
20. A good education.
21. He got married.
22. Love.
23. UFO's.
24. Wealth.
25. Drinking.
26. A bicycle—his first, in 1950.
27. "How old are you?"
28. Make a movie.
29. The Oscars.
30. His throat.

History

1. Maps. He was a mapmaker.
2. Kentucky.
3. Oranges.
4. Mobile, Alabama. In Mobile Bay.
5. Peru.
6. Sign the Constitution.
7. He was hurt. He'd spilled acid on his clothes.
8. Peanuts.
9. True. But reaction was so strong against it that it was removed from circulation.
10. He took a nap.
11. It was a face-slapping contest, and the two men now hold the world's record.
12. Butter. That was the invention of margarine.
13. The moon. From the Russian satellite Luna 3.
14. Tennis.
15. Disneyland.
16. Panama Canal.
17. The historic airplane flight by the Wright brothers.
18. The Tower of London. The crown jewels are there also.
19. Yes. Empress Nagako is Hirohito's wife.
20. Chewing gum.
21. Warm. He hated it. He switched beds continuously to keep cool.

Animal World

1. Yes. If you do not do it gently and carefully, he will be in a bad mood for the whole day.
2. His name. It says "Smokey" on his hat.
3. "Give a hoot, don't pollute."
4. Yes, it is.
5. No. Close, but not exactly the same.
6. No. Females have 'em too.
7. Kill the snake and keep it. It's important to identify it for the doctor.
8. He's in love. And he's calling his mate.
9. An Eskimo. Only Eskimos are allowed to kill a walrus.
10. Whales.
11. The walrus.
12. True. They love candy.
13. A gosling.
14. In the wild. Elephants seldom mate in zoos.
15. Sleep. No one knows why, but it's true.
16. Yes. They purr too.
17. Welcome. Their intentions are peaceful.
18. Yes.
19. No. They have a very low sex drive.

Music and Song

1. "I love you." "So be sure it's true when you say I love you, 'cause it's a sin to tell a lie."
2. "I get ideas, I get ideas."
3. Delightful.
4. "My girl." (Who could ask for anything more?)
5. "My heart stood still." By Rodgers and Hart.
6. The stars—to play.
7. *Love Story.*
8. Old-time religion.
9. All for the love of you.
10. The saxophone.
11. A string quartet.
12. Caruso.
13. The trumpet.
14. No. It's very difficult and often discourages children from musical training.
15. The instrument is called a triangle, too.
16. Yes. It screens out other noises.
17. Bach. It's one of his best-known works.

Sports, Games, and Hobbies

1. Raising tropical fish.
2. 300.
3. 500 feet.
4. The championship and a world record.
5. On his body. His silks is his riding outfit.
6. Weight lifting.
7. Tennis.
8. Jumping rope.
9. A golfer.
10. A silver arrow.
11. The heavyweight boxing championship of the world.
12. Helium.
13. Skiing. $1.5 billion.
14. Playing chess and losing to American champ Bobby Fischer.
15. Volleyball.
16. "A partner."
17. Yes, you can.
18. The strike zone.
19. By pinning his opponents' shoulders to the floor.
20. Playing volleyball.
21. Play badminton. She's the champ.
22. Tennis.
23. The Grand Canyon.
24. Olive oil.
25. Yes. It's very popular.
26. A matador.

Around The World

1. Pyramids.
2. True.
3. Yes. It is a legal punishment.
4. The Eskimos. It's their traditional sport.
5. Have a water chaser.
6. Yes. Four words (Aloha au, ia, oe.).
7. Get married. It's a prenuptial ritual.
8. On her hand.
9. They hiss.
10. Drinking water for the summer—35 gallons of it.
11. You'll be arrested and imprisoned from one week to two years.
12. Have a baby.
13. Sausage or wurst.
14. Bread.
15. Speaker of the House of Commons. The feigned reluctance is a century-old tradition.

16. Wigs. The Japanese get turned on by long, skinny necks and Audrey has one of those.
17. Political party conventions.
18. Every 6 months.
19. To see a play. It's the world-famous theater.
20. True.
21. In France.
22. Good luck. Danes even built nests for them.
23. Throw your lei overboard.
24. Worry.

Movies and Television

1. Several hundred wild monkeys, the descendants of the *Tarzan* cast.
2. Brains.
3. "The Mary Tyler Moore Show."
4. "Que sera, sera." She sings her famous song at the opening of each episode.
5. Shelly Winters.
6. Her umbrella.
7. The Shell People.
8. Courage.
9. Alice.
10. At the O.K. Corral in *Gunfight at the O.K. Corral.*
11. The seven dwarfs.
12. "Oh, Pancho!"
13. "Take it off, take it all off."
14. Language—offensive language.
15. *Gidget Grows Up.*
16. A disease.
17. Yes. And she was a good shot.
18. "This case is closed."
19. Her throne.
20. They were all wearing midis.
21. A silver bullet.
22. True.

Clip and Mail This Special Shipping Label and...

Let these Get-Ahead books help you write better, read faster, speak more effectively!

Here's an unusual opportunity for everyone who is determined to get ahead in business, socially or at school. Just print your name and address on the special shipping label printed on the opposite page. Clip it out and mail it together with the coupon below. We will paste your label on a package containing six valuable get-ahead books jam-packed with the powerful ideas, practical helps and short-cut steps you need for improving your writing, reading and speaking skills right now. These books cost $30.30 in their original hard-covers. Now, they're yours for only $6.25 in practical paperbacks. Here's a brief glimpse of what you get:

(1) Thesaurus
An authoritative guide to writing and speaking accurately. Thousands of major entries with synonyms listed by frequency of use.

(2) Faster Reading
Proven-successful ways to increase your reading speed and help you understand and remember more.

(3) Increase Your Vocabulary
How to expand your vocabulary quickly. 30-day new-word-mastery technique.

(4) Synonyms & Antonyms Dictionary
Provides exact words you need to express your written and spoken thoughts. Easy to use.

(5) Reference Guide
Leads you through the maze of almanacs, encyclopedias, atlases, manuals, and all other reference materials.

(6) Desk Dictionary
664 pages of clear, complete, up-to-date definitions, pronunciations, usages, origins of words. Illustrated.

MAIL THIS COUPON WITH SHIPPING LABEL NOW